A FLYFISHER'S REVELATIONS

A FLYFISHER'S REVELATIONS

Practical Tips, Strategies, and Wisdom

from Fifty Years Experience

ED VAN PUT

SKYHORSE
PUBLISHING

Skyhorse Publishing books may be purchased in bulk at special discounts for salespromotion, corporate gifts, fund-raising, or educational purposes. Special editions can also be created to specifications. For details, contact the Special Sales Department, Skyhorse Publishing, 307 West 36th Street, 11th Floor, New York, NY 10018 or info@skyhorsepublishing.com.

Skyhorse® and Skyhorse Publishing® are registered trademarks of Skyhorse Publishing, Inc.®, a Delaware corporation.

Visit our website at www.skyhorsepublishing.com.

10 9 8 7 6 5 4 3 2 1

Library of Congress Cataloging-in-Publication Data is available on file.

Print ISBN: 978-1-5107-8333-1

eBook ISBN: 978-1-5107-8334-8

Cover and interior design by Liz Driesbach
Drawings by Gordon Allen

Printed in China

BOOKS BY ED VAN PUT

The Beaverkill: The History of a River and Its People

Trout Fishing in the Catskills

The Beaverkill: The History of a River and Its People, 2nd Edition

The Remarkable Life of James Beecher

A Flyfisher's Revelations

FOREWORD

The "revelations" in this remarkable book are unique, true, and wise—and they will interest novice and expert alike. The author has nothing to sell or promote, no purpose but to share what knowledge he has earned by having fly-fished for trout for sixty years—forty of which while working as a fisheries professional. You will find no new fly patterns presented here, no new tying materials, no news about new space-age rod materials, no new exotic places to fish. What you will find here, though, may well change your fly-fishing life.

Ed Van Put has written two important historical books, "The Beaverkill" and "Trout Fishing in the Catskills," but this is his first book about the techniques and wisdom he has learned in his long experience on the water, in many of those years fishing every day of the trout season. From memory and from his detailed journals, Ed offers an invaluable picture of what has accounted for his great successes—and what has proved unsuccessful, and why. He is one of the half dozen finest trout fishermen I have ever seen or fished with.

Lee Wulff, whom he knew well and often fished with, called him a "predator," someone whose stealth, care, and knowledge of his quarry, animate much of his character in pursuit of trout with a fly. He is a superb caster—his line minimally in the air, low to the water, quietly delivered—and his approach is cautious and deft. Ed is a trained fisheries biologist and a lifetime specialist for the New York State Department of Conservation. Creel Census work was his first professional activity and his long days checking on what fly fishers had caught, on which rivers, at what time of day, how and on what flies, gave him special access to valuable information. He visited open areas and the new "catch and release" sections of most Catskill rivers and kept detailed journals, which he continued for many years about his own fishing. The accumulated wisdom from these journals is immense. Drawing on these records has led to the proven truths in this book.

I have heard many folk remark that the only fly Ed uses is the Adams. This is not entirely true, though this one pattern in various sizes and with minor adjustments has indeed accounted for the largest percentage of trout he caught on the dry fly over the course of his long experience. There are reasons for this—and the reasons are not that he is trying to prove something or win a one-fly contest. The simplicity of this is characteristic of other choices he has made: mostly he uses a glass rod or, occasionally, bamboo. He prefers a double-taper white line; he likes to make his own leaders, with carefully studied measurements. He has faith in the news a thermometer tells. Along with his Adams, he uses the Hair-wing Royal Coachman in some broken water because it is easier to see; he carries two wet-fly patterns and mostly fishes them on a two-fly rig. He presents at length what he has learned about the most effective construction of dry flies—their shape, proportions, profile, floatability. He shares his basic patterns of presentation. Throughout, Ed supports his more technical revelations with revealing—and sometimes amusing—anecdotes, like the time while creel checking in a no-kill section of the Willowemoc he saw a man a ways upstream catch and slip into his vest what he thought was a fish; the "offender" brought forth what he had caught—a white hat.

This book, which demystifies so much of the fly-fishing experience, could only have been written by a man with Ed's hard-earned personal experience. There is no dogmatic insistence of papal pronouncements, no self-agrandizement, no second or third-hand advice. Ed shares what he has learned—and chiefly stresses the central importance of fishing with confidence. The fruit of his sharing will surely help any flyfisher, of whatever level of skill, to learn and then do exactly that: fish with more confidence.

—NICK LYONS

CONTENTS

To my wife, Judy O'Brien, I dedicate this book,

for sharing in everything I do, for always being there,

and always being helpful.

ACKNOWLEDGMENTS

I would like to extend a special thanks to my son, Lee. I am grateful for his input and assistance, for his photography, for his preparation of the digital data and statistics taken from my handwritten diaries, and for his meticulous help in compiling the materials for this book.

I have been fortunate to have lived, since the 1960s, in the little hamlet of Livingston Manor, where the Willowemoc Creek flows through the heart of the town. The Willowemoc connects the lifeblood of the communities of Livingston Manor and Roscoe; each with its own fly shops and fishing stores, where a call-in can provide an angler all the information needed to prepare for a successful fishing trip. Not everyone in town fishes, but many will know when the Hendricksons or Shad Flies are hatching, and the trout are rising. News of a large fish being taken can be the talk of the town, whether at the barbershop, Peck's Market, the Jeff Bank, or the Post Office.

The late Kris Lee was honored in 2018 as a "Catskill Legend" by the Catskill Fly Fishing Center & Museum for her efforts in "allowing others to appreciate the richness of the Catskill rivers and streams" by photographing her husband, fishing writer Art Lee, over their many decades together. I would like to honor Kris as well, with her talents from a photo shoot taken some years ago that appear on the jacket cover and interior of this book; and extend my sincere thanks to Galen Mercer for providing the original slides.

And to Nick Lyons, for his friendship, help, and encouragement in bringing this work to fruition, I am thankful.

INTRODUCTION

I never thought I would write a book about my own trout fishing experiences, despite having spent the greater part of my life fishing for trout and seeking information about trout and trout fishing, both pragmatic and historical.

In 1996, Lyons & Burford published my book titled *The Beaverkill: The History of a River and its People*. Shortly after the publication Nick Lyons forwarded me a letter from a reader named Bob LeDonne, who wrote :

> *I enjoyed the book enormously. It tells me everything I ever wanted to know about the history of the Beaverkill. When I return there in April, it will be like visiting an old friend. The book is a unique treasure that will survive as long as the river itself. However, it is not the book I was anticipating from Ed Van Put. To use a cliché, he is a "living legend" among Catskill fly fishermen, and we really need to hear more from him about fly fishing the Catskill rivers. Anyone who achieves his reputation with a fly box that contains only half a dozen patterns definitely has one more book to write, and it should be about flies and fly fishing, advice and anecdotes, and all the wisdom he has gained from his years on the river.*

My vocation was in Fisheries Management, where I had spent forty years with the Bureau of Fisheries, one year with New York State's Conservation Department, and the next thirty-nine with New York State's Department of Environmental Conservation (DEC) after Governor Nelson Rockefeller signed legislation on April 22, 1970, celebrating the first Earth Day, that transformed the Conservation Department into the DEC. Thirty-three of these years were spent as a Principal Fisheries Technician.

In addition to a career in Fisheries, I developed a personal interest in learning about the history of trout fishing. A casual hobby grew into many years spent researching the trout-fishing history of the Beaverkill, in books, sporting journals, and antiquated newsprint. I searched the records of County Clerks' Offices, historical societies, and libraries all through the Catskills from Hancock to Kingston, from Margaretville to Ellenville and beyond.

A chance meeting at the Kingston Library with Catskill historian Alf Evers, author of *The Catskills: From Wilderness to Woodstock*, was educational and beneficial. Evers was encouraging and offered helpful advice about interlibrary loans, describing the process of how books and microform were borrowed from the New York State Library in Albany.

Along with my wife, Judy, I conducted research at the state library in Albany, and the New York Public Library in Manhattan, as well as the libraries of universities that maintained extensive collections of angling books and periodicals such as the Mann Library at Cornell University, Ithaca, New York and the Mudd Library at Yale University, New Haven, Connecticut.

I followed *The Beaverkill* with *Trout Fishing in the Catskills*, in 2007: a voluminous work on the history of trout fishing in one of America's earliest angling destinations by many of our best-known and earliest fly-fishermen, fly tyers, and rod builders.

I kept a fishing diary for fifty years, but never bothered doing anything with the data. At the end of each year, I put the diaries away and out of sight and all but forgot them except on rare occasions when I would revisit a particular year for one reason or another. I never totaled up any of the data. I believe aging and curiosity caused my recent decision to evaluate what I had spent a good portion of my life accumulating.

My review of a thirty-year period, from 1972 until 2001, was not only surprising and revealing, but also caused me to search for the reasons for my angling success, and this was the motivation for this book.

The book covers my fishing experiences from the very beginning – as a new young angler. I moved from New Jersey to Livingston Manor in the Catskill Mountains to be able to spend more time fishing for trout; and ultimately I landed a job with the NYS Conservation Department. One of the first duties of the job was conducting a creel census on the Willowemoc Creek, interviewing fishermen and collecting data on whether they had caught fish, what they caught them on, size of fish, conditions, and so forth. I met many flyfishers along the way and soon began keeping a personal diary of my own angling experiences.

There are chapters here devoted to dry flies, which include tips on how to tie a well-balanced fly, how to fish and present a dry fly or midge to a rising trout, or how to prospect with a fly when no rises are apparent. "Flies that Sink" covers the use of fishing with wet flies, nymphs, and streamers, and discusses how productive wet-fly fishing can be, despite the fact that many flyfishers today pass up this very successful method of catching trout.

A chapter on "Presentation and Fishing with Confidence" gives tips on how best to present the fly to the fish and improve your confidence in fishing. It also explains the rationale of anglers who believe it is not necessary to fish with the exact fly that is hatching in order to be successful, but rather to present the fly as delicately and perfectly as a natural fly.

I have chapters on my favorite fly, the Adams, with which I had the most success, and favorite places to fish, including the Delaware, or Big River. There is biological and environmental information on how to determine whether a trout is a hatchery-raised fish or a wild-born fish in "Wild vs. Hatchery Fish"; the importance of water temperature in "Take a Temperature for Trout"; and answers to such questions as "Do We Ever Catch the Same Fish Again."

Also covered in depth are techniques I've learned on how to fish—casting, position, timing, monitoring the trout and their rises, and other observations that have helped me along the way. Interestingly, since I began to write this book, I see things differently, and realize that my success in catching trout was not limited to just "the fly" or fishing an Adams–it's the culmination of such skills as how to cast accurately and well, to place the fly where you want it to be, to know where the fish are lying and where to position yourself, and to fish with confidence.

It is my wish to share my knowledge of trout fishing and to pass along helpful tips and information I've learned from my extensive experiences in fly-fishing.

1

FISHING WITH FLIES

*The statement that "a vital part of fly fishing is fly casting"
is not even debatable. One would expect to see on the streams,
lakes and ponds, casters in approximate numbers who are good,
bad and indifferent; but amazingly there are mighty few of each
of the two extremes and a vast army of the mediocre.*

CHARLES K. FOX, *Rising Trout* (1978)

My path into the world of fly-fishing was unconventional. No one in my family even fished, although kids in my neighborhood did on occasion fish local waters, and I went along with them from when I was about nine or ten years of age.

Perhaps I was also influenced by my grandfather, after whom I was named, although he was not a fisherman but a fish peddler, selling fish from the back of a small truck in Paterson, New Jersey. He would drive into New York City to the Fulton Fish Market to purchase fish, and then travel up and down the streets of Paterson, letting housewives know he had fresh fish to sell. It was he who encouraged me to fish and made me feel as though fishing was important, as he would eat anything I caught, mostly bluegill sunfish, and urged me to catch more.

There were no trout streams near where I started fishing; the closest river was the Passaic, which at one time had the distinction of being listed as one of the most polluted rivers in America. Where I lived, the Passaic was always discolored and you could never see the bottom, and because of this it was impossible to determine if the water was two feet deep or ten. It was wise to stay out of the river and fish from the bank. The Passaic of my youth contained large carp, eels, and golden shiners, which were known locally as "roach." We fished with dough balls made from bread for carp, but I don't remember any of us catching anything substantial except for a largemouth bass of about ten inches caught on a grasshopper. This event was the topic of conversation all summer.

There was also the Saddle River, which had its source in New York State near the New Jersey border and flowed southerly approximately sixteen miles through several communities in Bergen County. Along with other kids in the neighborhood I spent more time swimming and tubing in the river than fishing; the river had a soft bottom, was slow flowing, and often meandered. The water was not particularly cold in summer, but it was cleaner than the Passaic, and you could actually see the bottom.

I fished with a short five-foot bait-casting rod, and learned how to use it from other kids who also showed me how to put a worm on the hook and how to use split shot and a bobber. My lack of casting experience was obvious; it seemed as though every time I made a cast, I had to spend ten minutes untangling the backlash on the reel.

The only fish I ever caught in the Saddle River were catfish, also known as bullheads, although my first experience fishing for trout occurred on that river. One day, news spread through the neighborhood that Saddle River had been stocked with trout at a bridge crossing near where we used to fish and swim. The rumor indicated that trout were an important game fish and we hustled to the river on our bikes; when we arrived at the bridge, we quickly saw that the stocking rumor was true. There in a placid pool immediately upstream of the bridge was a school of trout, visibly swimming around together rather aimlessly, as if they did not know what to do or where to go. This is understandable; until that time they had spent their entire lives living in a pond at the hatchery. Even my inexperience told me this was an odd situation and fishing for these vulnerable fish was going to be like fishing in a barrel.

We all had similar rods and various skills in casting; we had brought worms for bait and although we could reach where the trout were, they ignored our baited hooks. We gave up after a reasonable period of time as we could tell these fish were not interested, and returned to our neighborhood where we learned that in order to catch the trout we needed to use liver for bait, because trout were fed chopped liver in the hatchery. Fishing with liver did not interest us, and so we passed on the trout and continued to use the river for skinny dipping and tubing.

During my teenage years, my family moved from Fair Lawn to the neighboring community of Hawthorne, and I was able to expand my fishing experiences and fished more regularly in a couple of nearby ponds, as well as in Pompton Lakes, a 175-acre manmade impoundment on the Ramapo River. I could reach the lake, about a nine-mile trip, by bicycle and rent a rowboat for about three dollars a day. The upper portion of the lake was fairly shallow and contained masses of lily pads and other underwater vegetation, along with an abundance of large bluegills, some ten and twelve inches in length, as well as pumpkinseed sunfish and a few largemouth bass.

The bluegills had a habit of feeding on the surface, and I noticed that some flies hovered over the water, moving up and down, and on occasion touched the water (most likely laying eggs). At the time I would not have known the difference between a mayfly and a caddisfly, but I noticed that when a fly landed on the surface, the bluegills rose to intercept it. This type of feeding occurred along the shoreline and in the shallower areas of the lake. Surface feeding was so prevalent that it caused me to think about fishing with flies.

I soon developed an interest in fly-fishing and decided to purchase a fly-rod. I found one in a local shop that sold "a little bit of everything." Located in a back corner of the store was a rod rack that held several bamboo fly rods; I picked out an 8 ½' rod, and gently moved it from side to side. This was the first time I had ever held a fly-rod and I can still remember the impression. I tried to envision what it would be like to fish with such a long and delicate rod, gently moving it back and forth; after feeling its suppleness, I imagined what it would be like to catch a fish on it. I was about thirteen years old and didn't know anyone who fly-fished. The rod was not a custom bamboo rod, but rather one that was mass-produced in Japan that sold for about fifteen or twenty dollars. I had no idea how to cast with it, having only seen photographs of fishermen holding fly rods rather than casting them.

I knew nothing about fly-fishing at the time, and fished warm-water lakes and ponds with a casting rod using bass plugs and spinners. I did take notice that there were flies, mainly along the shoreline, and that fish leaped from the water to catch them whenever they landed or came close to the surface–especially the large bluegills, which made a distinct noise as they inhaled the bug or fly.

A few days later, I visited the Paterson Rod & Gun store on West Broadway and bought an inexpensive reel, line, and leader. The store was owned by Jimmy Salvato, who was the popular outdoor columnist for the *Paterson Evening News*, and the father of champion fly-caster Joan Salvato (Wulff), who was then in her early twenties.

Being a complete novice, choosing from the large selection of flies in their individual little compartments was challenging. I selected a few dry flies that looked as though they would catch fish, and a small streamer that was probably designed after a Coachman wet fly. I could not even imagine how the flies were constructed, or what they were made with, although I did manage to teach myself how to cast, at least well enough that I had success with the bluegills, especially when sight-fishing for them in the shallows of Pompton Lakes. I later learned that fishing with flies for warm-water species, such as bluegills, calico bass, or crappies, yellow perch, large and smallmouth bass, was probably the most underutilized method of fly-fishing. Bluegills are a great fish to catch on a fly-rod; they are also abundant and are not very selective about the fly pattern.

My earliest efforts in fly-fishing began by casting where a rise had appeared and I would "nick" the water with the fly, a couple of times, then gently drop the fly at the same location. Often as soon as the fly landed a fish would take it, and the fun started. The reason for "nicking" the water was to imitate the natural flies dancing up and down over the water and dipping on the water's surface, depositing eggs. I thought "this is how you fly-fish," as I caught a lot of bluegills and roach or golden shiners.

If the fly was not taken immediately, I would give it movement, which often resulted in success; the action could be fast and furious, and the spirited bluegills on the end of a fly-rod were worthy opponents. They would turn their side to the rod, and their liveliness would suggest a fish that was twice as large as they were. Some of those bluegills in Pompton Lakes would top twelve inches, or slightly better on occasion.

I soon made several trips to the Paterson Rod & Gun store to buy more flies, and on one occasion Jimmy Salvato, apparently curious as to where I was fishing, asked, "What are you catching?" When I told him bluegills, he laughed, and responded irreverently "on trout flies?"

2

THE ROAD LESS TRAVELED

The first desideratum is to find time to go fishing. There is the rub in the case of most of us. We are so tied down to the pursuit of the essential dollar that we lose the best and most innocent pleasures that this old earth affords. Time flies so fast after youth is past that we cannot accomplish one-half the many things we have in mind, or indeed one-half our duties. The only safe and sensible plan is to make other things give way to the essentials, and the first of these is fly fishing.

THEODORE GORDON, *The Fishing Gazette*, August 20, 1904

During my teenage years I never fished for trout. There were stocked streams within reach, but at the time I didn't understand the philosophy of raising trout in hatcheries on unnatural foods, such as liver and pellets composed of fishmeal, plants, and various animal trimmings, then placing the trout in streams and trying to catch them. This seemed like bogus fishing, and so I continued to fish for bass and bluegills.

However, once I learned through books, newspapers, and outdoors magazines that there were streams and rivers that were also inhabited by trout that were actually born in the stream, and that trout streams were not all totally dependent on hatcheries, the idea of trout fishing became more appealing.

My interest in fly-fishing for trout increased, through reading *Field & Stream* and the fishing columns of A. J. McClane and Ted Trueblood, and everything else I could find about trout fishing. I began fishing the trout streams of northwestern New Jersey: the Pequest, Paulinskill, and Flat Brook, all tributaries of the Delaware River.

The first trout I ever caught was on Flat Brook, I took it on a dry fly named the Mosquito. The fly was tied with a stripped peacock eye quill body, pale grizzly hackle, and upright wings of pale grizzly hackle tips; its tail was of standard length, but was made with two pieces of fine monofilament (probably 7X) instead of hackle fibers. Although I had never fished dry flies for trout, the Mosquito looked as though it would catch fish.

1. The first trout I ever caught was on a Mosquito dry fly.

I began fishing in a nice-looking pool with good flow and depth along the opposite bank. Although there were no flies or rises apparent, and I had never fished a floating fly on flowing water, something told me to fish with a dry fly. A few false casts provided enough line to reach the head of the pool and gently place the fly on the surface film. I was fascinated by how realistic the Mosquito looked, and can still picture the fly sitting upright, high on the surface film, seemingly unattached to my leader. There was suspense as the fly drifted slowly back toward me. My eyes followed the fly and I was captivated by how life-like it appeared; my rod, line, and fly had created a scene that imitated nature. There was a splash, the fly disappeared, and I set the hook. After a short tussle I netted a brown trout of about nine inches and was quite pleased with the accomplishment. I liked the idea of dry-fly fishing. Everything was graphic. I was hooked.

It was also on Flat Brook that I really learned how to cast, and recognized that when you make a good cast a "message" is sent through the rod and into your arm letting you know that you are in control. Making a good cast produces a feeling similar to the sensation that comes from hitting a baseball squarely on a bat, resulting in a home run: the crack of the bat and the feeling you have confirms your success even before the ball clears the fence.

It was about this time that I also looked into tying my own flies and bought hooks, tying thread, fly-tying materials, and a book titled *Fly-Tying* by William Bayard Sturgis (1940) from Reed Tackle on Route 46 in Caldwell, New Jersey.

Through Jimmy Salvato's outdoor column "In the Great Outdoors" I read and learned about trout fishing in the Catskills: the run of large rainbow trout that migrated up the Esopus Creek in the spring, and of the brown trout of the Beaverkill, and that the Beaverkill was a great river for dry-fly fishing with abundant mayfly hatches and "plenty of room for a back cast."

These Catskill rivers were not much more than an hour's drive from my home at the time, and I began to travel by car up Route

209 to Route 28 and the Esopus. Too often the stream was high and turbid, the color of coffee. The dirty water was coming out of the portal from the Schoharie Reservoir; the "portal," an underground tunnel, transported water, usually muddy water, from the Schoharie Reservoir into the Esopus Creek and then to the Ashokan Reservoir. The Esopus looked unpleasant and unfishable, and I headed west to the Beaverkill downstream of Roscoe.

I caught my first Beaverkill trout in Cairns Pool on a dry fly that I had tied, known as an April Gray: the pattern called for grizzly hackle with a yellow wool body, ribbed with black tying thread, with a grizzly tail. The fly had no wings, which is why I chose it, as my fly-tying skills had not yet reached the level of being able to tie wings on a fly.

2. My first Beaverkill trout was caught on an April Gray.

I soon purchased another book titled *Flies*, by J. Edson Leonard (1960), which not only included better tying instructions but also a dictionary of 2,200 fly patterns. Tying flies looked difficult, but I was determined to learn because I did not want to be dependent on others, and I was anxious to learn more about fly-tying.

After a year or two of fishing weekends and holidays along the Beaverkill and Willowemoc, I contemplated moving to the region. I believe in the philosophy that one should work to live, not live to work; I wanted to live where, at the end of the work day, every day if possible, I could fish for trout and enjoy the scenic beauty of nature and the solitude and serenity that are often found along trout streams. Many of the rivers and streams flowed through the forest landscape of the Catskill Mountains, where 287,000 acres of forest preserve are owned by New York State and remain by law "forever wild."

Living close to the land also appealed to me, and the ecology of the Catskills, with its profusion of rivers and streams flowing through protected mountains and dense woodlands, was gratifying. I had looked into and fished in the Adirondacks, but the Catskills were not too far from my New Jersey roots and the great metropolis of Manhattan. In addition, the weather during the fishing season was milder in the Catskills than in the Adirondacks, which allowed for more fishing days, and thus began my relationship with fishing in the Catskills. This was in the early 1960s and, as many do, I commuted regularly each weekend and fished the Beaverkill, Willowemoc, and Delaware rivers, and found that I couldn't wait for Fridays.

Like many others I often stopped first at Harry and Elsie Darbee's Fly Shop. The Darbees operated a fly-fishing shop in a portion of their home which was a short walk to the Willowemoc Creek, between Livingston Manor and Roscoe. During the trout-fishing season patrons received more than just well-tied flies. The Darbees were a great source of information, that included which flies were hatching and which flies were "catching." They advised flyfishers on stream conditions, where to fish, and what to fish with.

Harry and Elsie had regular customers who would return after dark and share their fishing experiences of what their day was like. They swapped stories, and there were always a lot of trout caught over again, especially if they were large enough to boast about. Not surprisingly some fish grew faster in the shop than they did in the Beaverkill!

The conversation rarely strayed far from tackle, tactics, theories, books, or anything related to fly-fishing. The Darbees were teachers; Elsie would show you how to divide wood-duck wings on a Quill Gordon, and Harry would warn of the dangers of DDT. They shared their knowledge with anyone who was eager to learn; their lives, every day, revolved around fly-tying and fly-fishing.

Interspersed with his wisdom on how to catch trout, Harry would preach that the rivers and streams had to be protected and could not be taken for granted. Dam and road builders, gravel removers, and inadequate sewer plants and garbage dumps along the rivers were the enemy. He and Elsie fought everybody and anybody who would spoil or threaten the rivers and streams they loved. They fought for lower creel limits and "No Kill" water, and harassed state and local officials into doing their jobs by enforcing regulations that stopped the degrading of trout streams.

In 1965 I moved to the Catskills permanently and became one of the Darbees' neighbors; I rationalized that if it didn't work out, I could always return to New Jersey. Over the years, I spent a lot of time at their place; we sometimes fished together, drank, ate, and argued, and I became educated. Elsie died in 1980; Harry did not last long without her and passed less than three years later.

Fortunately, after moving to the Catskills, my fly-tying skills improved through the kindness of the Darbees; as well as that of Walt and Winnie Dette. The Dettes were also well-known Catskill fly-tyers who maintained a fly shop in their home along the Willowemoc Creek, a short distance upstream of Junction Pool, in the hamlet of Roscoe.

After improving my skills at the fly-tying vise, I began to tie flies with wings. This added to the number of trout flies that I carried. I purchased a copy of Ernie Schwiebert's *Matching the Hatch* and began tying some of the dry-fly patterns that were featured. *Matching the Hatch* had an appealing assortment of dry and nymph patterns, as well as spent or spinner patterns.

Though Schwiebert suggested trimming the hackle top and bottom on a number of the spent patterns, I could not make myself alter good dry-fly hackle by cutting it off the top and bottom of the fly. I didn't want the flies to float in the surface film, but rather on the surface film. The flies floated better when not trimmed and their silhouette was improved. In addition, on windy or breezy days, the spent wings could also catch a little breeze and rock the fly ever so slightly, at times just enough to imitate a live insect, which on occasion got the attention of a hungry trout.

I never believed it was necessary to directly imitate the various hatches, but I liked tying many of the patterns, and assumed that by carrying multiple flies they might come in handy. From the beginning of my fly-fishing experiences, I saw no evidence that rationalized directly imitating the fly that was on the water. Once I learned of the abundance and variety of the mayfly, caddis, and midge species, I could not justify the concept that it was necessary to match the great variety of aquatic insects that inhabited a trout stream; trout fishing just couldn't be that technical or complicated. More often than not there were multiple flies hatching at the same time, and the flies did not take turns departing the stream like airplanes on an airport runway. With several hatches occurring at once it was difficult to determine which flies the trout were taking.

Inside my fly boxes I had flies that matched particular hatches, as well as standard fly patterns that did not. Interestingly, right from the beginning I had more success with fly patterns that did not imitate anything specific in nature, such as the Adams, Royal Wulff, Pheasant-Tail Midge, and Chuck Caddis dry flies. And my choice of using fewer rather than more dry flies increased when I began recording my trout fishing in a diary.

3

CREEL CENSUS AND THE DEPARTMENT OF ENVIRONMENTAL CONSERVATION

The New York State Department of Environmental Conservation's mission is to conserve, improve and protect New York's natural resources and environment and to prevent, abate and control water, land and air pollution, in order to enhance the health, safety and welfare of the people of the state and their overall economic and social well-being.

MISSION STATEMENT OF THE NYS DEC

It was at the Darbees' fly shop that I first met William H. Kelly, a fisheries biologist with the New York State Conservation Department. "Kelly," as we always fondly called him, was also a knowledgeable fly-fisherman who, in addition to his passion for trout fishing, enjoyed fishing for shad with a fly rod.

A couple of years after I had moved to Livingston Manor, Kelly asked if I would be interested in working in Fisheries for the Conservation Department. He explained that I would be participating in a two-year study of the Willowemoc Creek that included the seven-mile stretch between the hamlets of Livingston Manor and Roscoe.

This portion of the Willowemoc is the most prolific, and consists of excellent trout habitat, with numerous large pools, and lengthy riffles containing an abundance of aquatic insects and various minnow species. I was eager to work on the census, as I lived along the Willowemoc Creek, and the Beaverkill and Willowemoc were familiar waters. I knew what my fishing was like on these rivers and now I had an opportunity to compare my successes and failures with others.

There were several reasons for the survey, which occurred in 1969 and 1970: one was to evaluate the impact of the recently completed construction of the Route 17 Quickway. There had been environmental concerns about the new highway and the extensive stream disturbances that took place and how they would affect the ecosystems of the two rivers. Concerted efforts were made by organized sportsmen to keep the highway from following along the banks of the Beaverkill and Willowemoc and crossing back and forth with multiple bridges.

Trout fishermen were angry that huge amounts of earth were mined from hastily developed gravel pits, too close to the rivers, and they wondered about the long-term effects that the temporary and permanent bridges that were built every couple of miles would have on the fisheries and the aquatic insect population. Organized sportsmen, such as The Beaverkill-Willowemoc Rod and Gun Club, the Sullivan County Federation of Sportsmen's Clubs, and the Theodore Gordon Flyfishers opposed the construction of the highway so close to the rivers, and they lobbied for the highway to be placed further away from the Beaverkill and Willowemoc Creek.

Concerns also included erosion and siltation problems, along with additional highway runoff of salt, sand, and the possibility of oil spills. Drainage ditches were constructed, paved with asphalt to lead the water off of the highway quickly and into the Willowemoc and Beaverkill. (In the end, the new Route 17 was constructed where it was designed to go, and a four-lane highway with higher speed limits was added to the already existing two lanes of Old Route 17.)

Another purpose for the census was to collect data on the recently established Catch-and-Release ("No Kill") special-regulation fishing area on approximately two miles of the Willowemoc Creek. There had been a catch-and-release section designated on the lower Beaverkill a couple of years earlier that was highly successful and had become extremely popular with fly-fishermen.

The regulation stated that anglers were permitted to fish with artificial lures only, such as flies, spoons, and spinners. No live bait was allowed, and all trout had to be released back into the water unharmed. The trout that were released grew, with many holding over through the winter. The following season they were three or four inches larger than when they were first stocked. The regulation kept more mature trout in the river that would possibly spawn, and thereby increase the wild trout population. The "special regulation" areas quickly became popular with anglers, who were assured that there were trout in those sections of the river all season long, not just when the river was stocked in the spring.

A typical census day began at 7:00 a.m. and lasted until anywhere between 7:00 and 9:00 p.m., depending on the fishing pressure. There was no overtime pay, and my schedule included weekends and holidays, as those were days when fishing pressure was highest. The census involved a count run every two hours along the river, recording the number of anglers seen fishing between Livingston Manor and Roscoe. During the time between the count runs I interviewed anglers and then recorded the data.

The interview included questions such as where the anglers were from, what time they had begun fishing and what they were fishing with, such as bait, lures, or flies. If any trout were caught and kept outside the "No Kill" area, I would examine them to determine whether they were wild, hatchery, or holdover fish, and also measure and weigh them. A scale sample was taken for age-growth analysis.

Although I would spend many fourteen-hour days interviewing fishermen and gathering data, there were occasions when fishing pressure was low, which enabled me to spend time observing the trout themselves. To amuse myself I would watch for a fish that was high in the water column and feeding on the surface, occasionally rising to take a fly, ant, or beetle that came floating along.

My approach to the fish would be careful, and when I was close enough and the trout was not spooked I would pick up a pea-sized pebble, choke cherry, tiny bud, or anything else that was small enough to toss and penetrate the water in front of the feeding trout. If the object landed right in front of the trout, invariably the item would be seized immediately by the feeding fish, and then expelled. This came as a revelation; it revealed the predatory instincts of the trout and the reflexive instincts that trout maintain.

My toss had to be accurate and close enough to the fish, so that as soon as the object hit the water directly in front of the trout, it was instinctively seized. The fish would not fall for the hoax a second time. I repeated this many times, though if I tossed the item a little more upstream of where the trout was located and it had a better chance to look it over as it drifted downstream, the object would not be taken. It seemed to work only when the item was close to the rising trout and the fish had to act quickly. This is understandable; if the trout doesn't act quickly, food passes it by. I learned to use this knowledge when fishing with wet flies, often dropping the fly right in front of the feeding trout and quickly giving the fly motion, which generally produced a strike.

One of the more interesting things I learned was that when there was a prolific hatch and the trout were working well on the surface, flyfishers caught trout on a variety of fly patterns and not necessarily on direct imitations of the fly that was hatching.

I also learned that anglers who parked their cars close to the river and focused their fishing within sight of their vehicles did not do as well as those anglers who were willing to walk to areas where there was less fishing pressure.

During the census I was able to meet a great many fly-fishermen and look at numerous trout flies. I never asked to see the flies, my job was just to record whether they were fishing with flies, lures, or bait; however, fly-fishermen often wanted to show me the flies that they were using, especially if they were having success. This aspect of the census was enlightening because their flies also varied greatly. One of the first lessons I learned was that you could have ten people show you a Light Cahill, and you might have ten different versions of the Light Cahill. Not everyone's Light Cahill looked the same: some were lighter, others darker, and there was also a great variation in the quality of the flies and the materials used to make them. Many flies were overdressed with hackle, and their proportions were inconsistent.

The Hendrickson hatch is a favorite on the Beaverkill watershed and because of the fly's abundance the trout at times feed with uncontrolled recklessness and reach a point where they seem to take anything that drifts by. There were days when Hendricksons covered the water and everyone was catching trout, but not necessarily using a Hendrickson imitation. Some were catching trout on a Royal Wulff, others a Dun Variant or an Elk-Hair Caddis.

I might add that creel census was not always an enjoyable event. As a representative of the Conservation Department there were times when I would receive anglers' complaints about everything the State of New York was doing wrong. "The fishing is not as good as it used to be," "Why don't you stock bigger fish," "Where did you stock? I bought a license and you have to tell me!" and "The state should stop issuing so many doe permits."

I've always recognized that I had pretty good vision; at times I could see flies or rises that other people I fished with could not. I attributed my success in fishing partially to this, as once during an eye exam the ophthalmologist told me that my vision was 20/15, which is better than the standard of 20/20.

While making a count run of anglers fishing between Livingston Manor and Roscoe I noticed a fly-fisherman at Sherwood Flats. He was fishing a short line, and I assumed he was nymphing. As I was watching I saw the fisherman strike and set the hook. I decided to pull the car to the side of the road as I saw him bring up a fish that was wiggling on the end of his line. He used his net and as he lifted it, I could see the fish's white belly as it was struggling to get off the hook. He removed it from the net, looked upstream and down, and then slipped the fish into his fishing vest. This was the "No Kill" area, and although there was some distance between us, I had a good vantage point.

Usually, if I saw violation–anglers keeping fish in the "No Kill"— I would ask to see their fishing license and jot down their contact information. I would then notify the local Conservation Officer and give him the information so that he could contact the fisherman. However, my supervisor did not like me getting involved with legal issues because it took me away from what I was supposed to be doing, counting and interviewing anglers.

I had never witnessed such a blatant violation as this. I crossed the river downstream where he could not see me, and walked up behind him. As I got closer I noticed he had a couple of patches from T.U. (Trout Unlimited) and other fishing organizations on his vest, and he didn't look like the average poacher. When I said hello, I must have had a big smirk on my face, as I had caught him red-handed. He immediately responded, "I guess you want to see my license?"

He handed me his license, and then I said triumphantly "and now I want to see the fish you put in your vest pocket!" He reached into his vest and, with a sheepish look on his face, pulled out a whitish-colored woolen hat band filled with flies! He explained "this came floating down river. I hooked it, and looked around to see if anyone was upstream or downstream that could have lost it, and seeing no one, I put it in my vest pocket." I not only was embarrassed but now had to face my supervisor and explain why I had lost valuable time. I would have sworn in court that this angler had hooked a trout and kept it. I apologized to the fisherman and he said, "That's OK, if it was someone who did keep a fish, you would have caught him!"

My job on the Willowemoc census was the beginning of a forty-year career with the Bureau of Fisheries.

When I began working in fisheries a large portion of our work was accomplished outdoors in the field, participating in stream and lake surveys. I also spent a significant amount of time working in Habitat Protection and the Protection of Waters Regulatory Program, also known as Article 15 of the Stream Protection Law, which required a permit for any disturbance to the bed or banks of classified streams.

However, most of my time was spent as a Principal Fish & Wildlife Technician, and while I participated in fisheries surveys and fish collections on individual streams, rivers and lakes, the majority of my time was spent purchasing Public Fishing Rights on trout streams.

Public Fishing easements allow the public the right to fish in and along the streams and rivers on private land, usually 33 feet from the water's edge. In addition to the Public Fishing easements, we acquired angler parking areas as well as foot paths to access the easements. The only activity allowed on these easements was fishing; no other activity is lawful: no swimming, hiking, picnicking, hunting, or the like. New York State began the PFR program throughout the state back in the 1930s to preserve public fishing. Today the vast majority of open water along streams and rivers is made possible because of the Public Fishing Rights program.

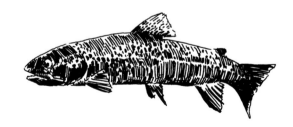

4

THE ANGLER DIARIES

I began using a diary when I started working for the Conservation Department's Bureau of Fisheries in 1969. Fish and Wildlife employees spent a large portion of their obligations in the field and were expected to keep a daily diary to record the details of their daily activities, including the location and time spent on the assignment. The diary was then used as a reference for timecards with coded activities that were turned in every two weeks.

There were also years when the Bureau of Fisheries participated in an angler diary program on certain streams, rivers, lakes, and ponds to collect additional fisheries data directly from those anglers who fished the waters being studied. Anglers who volunteered were

supplied with a small seasonal diary that was collected at the end of
the fishing season and then analyzed by biologists.

Our regional office was located in New Paltz, in Ulster County;
and the region encompassed seven counties and a sizable portion of
the Catskills, as well as a large section of the Hudson and Delaware
rivers. There were days when we were sent to the Hudson River, at Con
Edison's Indian Point nuclear power plant, to respond to a fish kill in
the morning; and that same afternoon traveled to the Delaware River
watershed at Callicoon, to meet with a farmer who had an erosion
problem along the North Branch of Callicoon Creek.

Many of our work activities were accomplished outdoors, participating in fieldwork that included collecting various biological and
physical data relative to fish production. We collected fish, estimated
fish populations, recorded species, sizes, weights, and took scale
samples for age/growth analyses, which helped determine growth
rates. A fish's age is determined by studying growth rings on the scale.
The trout scales also provided further information as to whether the
fish was of hatchery origin, or was born in the stream and was known
as a "wild" trout. We conducted water chemistries, temperatures,
and took flow samples. Flow samples are recorded in cubic feet per
second, and calculated as follows: the stream section, usually at least
10 feet, is marked off with stakes and string. The width of the stream
is measured, and three depths of water are taken across the stream
and averaged. A float is used and timed with a stopwatch from the
moment it enters the section until it passed underneath the line at the
end of the section. This is done three times, and an average is taken.
The flow is calculated by multiplying the width times the average
depth by the product of the distance and time. The result represents
cubic feet per second of flow. We used a variety of information to
assess the health and condition of the stream or body of water we
were investigating.

Field surveys were important, and often decided whether a stream
should be stocked, or whether existing populations were adequate

enough that stocking was no longer necessary; we also analyzed if special fishing regulations were needed to protect and improve existing fish populations.

I've always enjoyed statistics and viewed keeping an angler diary as something that might provide information that could have an influence on my own fishing experiences. I not only recorded the fish I caught, but also the emergence dates of the fly hatches that were familiar. Did the Shad Fly appear in April or May? When did the Green Drakes hatch–at the end of May or the beginning of June? What was the date when Judy caught that 20-inch trout when there were so many Green Drakes in the air and on the water on the lower East Branch? Once you experience what is often an incredible number of Green Drakes and Coffin Flies on the water during that hatch, you'll want to commit those dates to memory. And finally, would I witness a change in the structure of trout populations?

I also contemplated whether I would catch more or fewer wild trout in the future, and if they would be larger or smaller fish. I thought it would be fun to be able to look back and remember specific days, unusual catches, and other incidents. There were veteran fly-fishermen who had complained about the lack of wild trout, and a number of anglers who grumbled about the lack of large fish, and claimed that fishing was "not as good as it used to be." All of these issues were of interest, and could possibly be answered by keeping an angler diary.

In 1970 I began recording my angling experiences, although it was not until two years later that I included which fly I caught trout on, the origin of the trout, whether they were wild, stocked, or holdovers. At this time I had no favorite fly patterns, and subscribed to the idea of using dry flies that were "near enough" to what was on the water in size, shape, (silhouette) and color. Size referred to hook size; shape referred to flies tied either with upright wings like mayflies, or with wings tied over the body like caddisflies or stoneflies; and color was not exact, but rather light, medium, or dark.

At times I recorded water temperatures, as well as the fly hatches that I recognized. I really knew little about fly species other than being able to tell mayflies from caddisflies, stoneflies, and midges. However, I was accurate with my recordings as they related to the sizes, quantities, and origin (wild or hatchery) of the trout, and what fly the trout were caught on. My descriptions of the hatches, however, were not always accurate with regard to the species, as there were a great many times when several species of flies hatched at the same time, and I didn't believe a specific species of fly was that important.

Each day that I fished I recorded where I was fishing, what was caught, and the fly and hook size the trout were taken on. I would also make notes about unusual events, stream flows, and water temperature, if important. A typical diary entry would look like the following:

October 13, 1974, Fished Willowemoc Creek "No Kill Area" (Power Enclosure), the "No Kill" area allowed year-round fishing, there was very little spawning in the Willowemoc in the "No Kill" area and collecting young of the year was rare which indicated there was little spawning success. Caught 7 hatchery brown trout, 2 holdover brown trout, 1 wild rainbow trout on Adams #18. River low and perfectly clear. Good hatch of #16 & #18 light wing duns, olive body, same fly that's been hatching on Beaverkill and Delaware. Caught many of the fish on the first cast. All the hatchery fish were good size 12"-13," two holdovers slightly larger. Do the more colorful holdovers go up stream and spawn? This is the third rainbow I caught in the Power Enclosure this season, can we be getting some spawning? Beautiful time to fish, lots of duns. Rainbow fought really well and in excellent condition.

Another example:

June 3, 1976, Fished Delaware River (Dark Eddy), Caught 5 wild S.T. (speckled or brook trout), 1 – 6" 1 - 10" 1 – 10 ½" 1 – 11" 1 – 12." Caught 2 wild R.T. (rainbow trout) 1 – 10" 1 – 13," caught 1 hatchery B.T. (brown trout) 10 ½" all on #12 Adams. Lots of #12 dk. dun caddis with green egg sac. Tremendous numbers of Coffin Flies. Fished from 5:30 to 9:30 PM. Fish not really rising, few large stone flies.

And another:

April 28, 1973, Fished Delaware River (Dark Eddy) Caught 4 wild R.T. (rainbow trout) 2 – 14 ½" 1 – 15" 1 – 16" Adams #14, Terrific hatch, Hendricksons, two types of caddis, 1 #14 very light. Very cold & rainy. Flies riding surface sideways, upside down, Probably because of rain. Fished from 3 pm to 7 pm. Fish worked well, hatch ran into 7 pm. Flies came down upright when rain eased up. Even caddis were upside down having trouble getting off. H2O 50 degrees, air probably 40 degrees. Matt left fly in canoeist on back cast (and didn't know it.)

Once I began keeping a diary I found that it was necessary to carry a pencil and a slip of paper; I carried these in the first tray of my FYE chest fly box along with streamers and bucktails. I first saw this type of fly box in 1969 while doing the creel census along the Willowemoc Creek. The fly box was quite popular with those who fished the Willowemoc and Delaware, as it was handmade in Osceola Mills, PA. The chest fly box was ideal for those who did not like bulky vests filled with boxes of flies; it enables your arms to move freely and does not interrupt your casting stroke. The box is strapped just above the top of your waders; if you waded too deeply and started taking on water you needed to back up if you wanted to keep your flies dry. I've used this chest fly box for more than fifty years, and the only thing I had a problem with were the straps, as I wore out a couple of pair over the years. All of my flies were in one conveniently located and easily accessible fly box!

At the end of each season, I put the diaries away and rarely ever looked inside; however, I recently decided to review the diaries from 1972-2001 and interpret the contents, and have given a great deal of

4. The FYE Chest fly box I have used for more than 50 years.

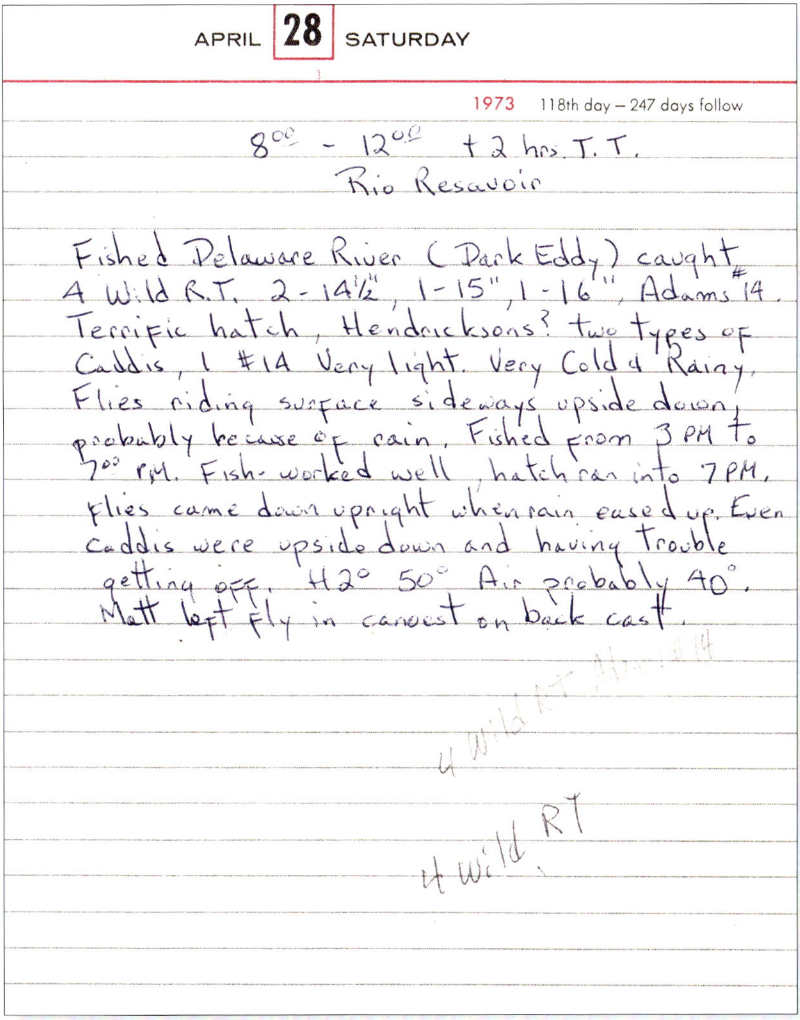

APRIL **28** SATURDAY

1973   118th day – 247 days follow

8⁰⁰ - 12⁰⁰ + 2 hrs. T.T.
     Rio Resavoir

Fished Delaware River (Dark Eddy) caught
4 Wild R.T. 2-14½", 1-15", 1-16", Adams #14.
Terrific hatch, Hendricksons? two types of
Caddis, 1 #14 Very light. Very Cold & Rainy.
Flies riding surface sideways upside down,
probably because of rain, Fished from 3 PM to
7⁰⁰ PM. Fish worked well, hatch ran into 7 PM,
flies came down upright when rain eased up. Even
Caddis were upside down and having trouble
getting off. H2° 50° Air probably 40°.
Matt left fly in canoest on back cast.

4 Wild RT Hen #14

4 wild RT

4 Wild.

3. Sample diary entry, April 28, 1973.

thought to the fact that I've caught a lot of trout on just a few different
fly patterns. It was never my goal to prove or disprove anything by
using a minimal number of dry flies. In the beginning I tended not to
change flies because I was somewhat influenced by keeping a diary–as
each time I changed a fly, I needed to stop fishing and make notes for

later entries. I became somewhat hesitant about changing flies and got in the habit of stalling before doing so.

Often, when fishing, it was just easier to keep the same fly on and remember the number of trout caught, than to change flies and have to stop and record that one was caught on this, and three on that. My focus was more on catching trout on the fly I was using; and my fishing improved by concentrating more on casting and presentation, as I did not need to waste time changing flies. While some anglers may look at this as a handicap, I am certain that it contributed to my becoming a better fly-fisherman. I tried to shy away from these types of instances: I wanted to keep things simple and I had great success and confidence in the Adams and a few other dry flies.

Early on my selection of dry flies included patterns like the Adams, Pheasant-Tail Midge, Royal Wulff or Hair-Winged Royal Coachman. I believed in these flies, and learned there was no need to use others unless I wanted to, not because I had to. This may be difficult for some anglers to accept, but I've recorded an accurate account of my fishing experiences for more than fifty years.

Practically all of the diary entries refer to trout fishing in the Catskills, with a visit every once in a while to the New York section of the Battenkill, and the West Branch of the Ausable in the Adirondacks. Primarily the data was gathered on streams in the Delaware River watershed such as the Beaverkill, Willowemoc Creek, Neversink, Delaware, and the East and West Branches of the Delaware River; and also in the Hudson River watershed, and included occasional trips to the Esopus, Schoharie, and Rondout Creeks.

I always carry a tape measure in my fishing vest, and while it was used on occasion on most waters if I caught a large or interesting trout, I measured every trout caught on the Delaware for my own interest. There were also times when I would remove a few scales from a trout for age/growth analysis; I was curious to learn as much as I could about the river's fisheries and spent an enormous amount of time fishing the "big river." The Delaware was the largest and the most challenging water, and the most rewarding if you were successful. I thought of the Delaware as the "major leagues" as it was not easy wading or fishing, and catching double-digit numbers of trout on a trip to the river didn't happen often.

Every year I recorded my trout fishing experiences and I was certainly aware that at some point I began using fewer fly patterns when fishing with a dry fly; however, while I knew I was having success with just a few patterns I had no idea how significant this approach turned out to be until I totaled the yearly recordings from my angling diaries.

The angler diaries reveal that more trout were caught on dry flies than wet flies, nymphs, or bucktails and streamers. I caught a total of 12,167 trout on various flies during a thirty-year period from 1972 to 2001. However, there were years when I caught more trout on wet flies than dry flies. Overall, 76% of my trout caught were from four patterns.

While some years were better than others, I took a total of 6,668 brook, brown, and rainbow trout on dry flies during the thirty-year period. Of the 6,668 trout caught on dry flies I caught 86% of them on four different dry flies; I took 4,783 (72%) on an Adams. The Pheasant-Tail Midge and the Chuck Caddis netted 5.6% and 5.8% respectively, and I took 223 or 3.3% on a Royal Wulff. None of these four fly patterns are direct imitations of any particular aquatic insect. During this period, the remaining 901 trout were caught on various dry flies, averaging about thirty trout per year that were taken on miscellaneous fly patterns.

The greatest number of trout caught on dry flies in one season occurred in 1986, and numbered 638. During that season my diary reveals that 92.3% of the trout caught on dry flies were caught on two flies, the Adams (420) and Chuck Caddis (169). During the entire season only five other fly patterns were used; four were midge patterns, the Pheasant-Tail (11), Red (3), Green (1) and Badger Quill Midge (25), along with a Black Ant (9).

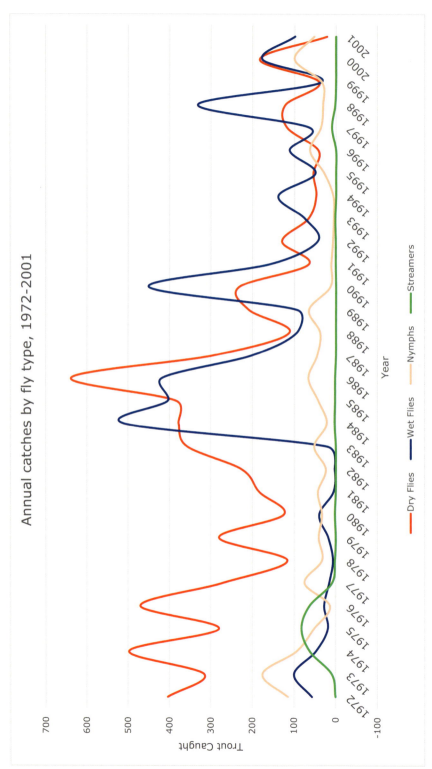

Annual catches by fly type, 1972-2001

— Dry Flies — Wet Flies — Nymphs — Streamers

5.

Variety of patterns & sizes used 1972-2001

Number of patterns used

5.

7. The Chuck Caddis dry fly was one of the four best-producing flies I fished with.

The second highest season was 1974, when I caught 497 brook, brown, and rainbow trout on nine different dry flies; the largest number again I took on the Adams, with 465 or 93.6%. I caught the other 32 trout on eight different dry flies including a Flying Caddis Fly, Gray Fox Variant, Coffin Fly, Little Sulphur Dun, Rat-Faced McDougal, Royal Coachman Bivisible, Pheasant-Tail Midge, and Katterman. What is interesting and perhaps thought-provoking is that it took one fly pattern to catch 465 of the 497 trout, and eight different patterns to catch 32 trout!

Of the trout caught on an Adams, I took one-half, or 51% on a size #14 hook, with 30% taken on a #16 hook, 14% on a size #18, and the remaining 4.2% taken on sizes #12 and #20. The Pheasant-Tail Midge accounted for 37 trout, and of these, 70% were caught on a size #22 hook, 26% on a size #20 hook, and the remaining 4% taken on a size #18 hook. The Royal Wulff accounted for 223 trout, with the most popular size being a #14, at 79%, and a #12 at 20%. As with the Adams and Pheasant-Tail Midge, the Royal Wulff imitates nothing specific in nature. The fly is similar to the Royal Coachman, a fly that has long been a conundrum to those who believe in direct imitation or

8A and 8B. A Royal Coachman dry fly and a Royal Wulff dry fly, flies similar in color with different tails.

matching the hatch. The Royal Wulff is a good "searching" or attractor pattern, and I primarily used it when there were no apparent rises and the fishing is slow. The fly is more effective in fast water where trout react quickly or the food passes them by. The Royal Wulff not only floats well, but its white wings make it easy to see and follow in fast water, an added benefit, especially on a windy day when the fly may not land exactly where you want it to.

When fishing with these particular fly patterns, if trout were rising I used an Adams; if the trout were feeding on Chironomids (midges) a Pheasant-Tail Midge; and if there was nothing visibly happening, I prospected with a Royal Wulff and focused more in the riffle areas.

I learned from my diary experiences that there are times when having too many flies to choose from made fly-fishing more complicated than it is. Carrying fewer flies can make one a better flyfisher because having less to choose from concentrates your efforts more on presentation, fly-casting accuracy, and tying or buying the best flies possible.

5

WILD VS.
HATCHERY TROUT

A hatchery trout may resemble a wild fish, but a
wild fish will never look like a hatchery trout.

WILLIAM H. KELLY III, NYS DEC Fisheries Biologist

We all have varying views of what makes our angling experiences enjoyable. Many years ago, I had a conversation with
Bob Darbee, brother of Harry Darbee, about a large rainbow trout
Bob had caught in Catherine Creek, a Finger Lakes tributary famous
for its annual spring migration of wild rainbow trout that run out of
Seneca Lake. Bob recalled the excitement of catching the big trout
followed by the immediate disappointment when he netted the fish
and noticed the rainbow was tagged. The tag was placed on the fish
by the Conservation Department and was undoubtedly captured
in the stream or lake and then was released as part of a study. Bob
expressed dismay that someone had previously handled his fish, and
he believed his fishing experience had been compromised.

At the time I thought Bob was over-reacting somewhat, but several years later while fishing the East Branch of the Delaware River upstream of Margaretville, I caught a 12" wild brown trout that had a plastic tag attached to its jaw. The tag read "caught and released by _____," with the name and address of the person who tagged the fish. I was upset that someone would cause discomfort to a wild fish by attaching a plastic tag to its jaw that may have interfered with its feeding and at the very least may have become a burden. Before releasing the trout, I snipped off the tag. I was also annoyed, wondering what the person had been thinking–was I supposed to feel obligated to this particular person for putting this trout back so that I could catch it? And, like Bob, I didn't like the idea that someone else had handled my fish. However, most everyone who fishes for trout seriously knows there is a good chance that the fish they caught may have been caught and released by someone else, or that the trout came from a hatchery and was obviously handled by someone prior to being released into the wild.

When I was first employed by the Conservation Department, I learned to tell the difference between wild and hatchery-reared trout. My supervisor, Bill Kelly, once stated that "a hatchery trout may resemble a wild fish, but a wild fish will never look like a hatchery trout."

Many contemporary flyfishers are more aware of our natural stream environment and the life cycles of trout than their predecessors were. Their knowledge extends beyond just wanting to catch fish than it was just a couple of decades ago, especially since the inception of regulations that require the fish to be returned to the water unharmed, such as in the "No Kill" Catch and Release areas on the Beaverkill and Willowemoc. Today it is more common to hear a fellow fly fisher state that they have caught a "nice wild brown" of a certain length. Their declaration is usually followed by a comment on how beautifully colored the fish was, with characteristic bright red spots and golden yellow sides, and that the fish fought like a wild trout. But how can it best be determined whether a trout is of wild or hatchery origin?

While color may contribute to identifying a trout's origin it should not be the only observation when determining whether or not a trout is a wild fish. The external appearance of brown trout can be influenced by several important factors: namely, food, environment, and life history.

The coloration of trout, both externally and internally, is influenced by diet; it is believed that red spots brighten, and pink flesh increases when trout are exposed to a diet of crustaceans, such as shrimp or scuds, crayfish, daphnia (small planktonic crustaceans), and snails.

Scientists tell us that the dark pigment cells in a trout's skin are controlled by the fish's eye, and trout are able to change color to a degree to match their backgrounds.

Trout that reside in tannic streams, with soft, silt-laden bottoms, are generally dark colored; and trout from large lakes, silvery, with brown or black spots. Those living in clear, transparent water with gravel bottoms are typically brightly colored, many with intense red spots surrounded by white halos.

Trout originating from different rivers, streams, or regions show considerable individual diversity, and the coloration can vary greatly. Brown trout can be blackish or silvery, or a beautiful golden brown with yellow and white undersides. Spots may be red, black, or brown, and can be round, stellate, or haloed, and vary in size, number and pattern.

Perhaps the most important influence on the external appearance of a wild brown trout is the fact that American brown trout were the result of the combination of several different subspecies associated with particular regions and drainage basins, each with different life history forms.

The fact that the first shipment of brown trout eggs came from Germany is well known; however, even the first shipment contained the eggs of two distinct forms of brown trout, and these were quickly followed by several others from Europe, including other regions of Germany, England, and Scotland. All are part of the present genetic makeup of American brown trout.

In the words of eminent trout fisheries biologist Dr. Robert J. Behnke, "Depending on the time of introduction and the hatchery source, the brown trout stocked around North America represented a range of genetic diversity. Natural selection operating in new environments has likely produced an array of differentiation so that hardly any two populations of American brown trout are exactly alike."

The surest way to identify a wild trout from a hatchery-reared trout is to examine the fish's scales under a microscope, as biologists and field technicians do in the laboratory. However, an angler can become familiar with determining a trout's origin on the stream by looking at the fins–particularly the pectorals, which are located on each side of the fish just behind the head. In general, the pectorals of hatchery-reared trout are deformed, often with the first spine or ray being bent, causing a misshapen, frayed, and broader appearance than the pectoral fin of a wild trout.

9. A wild brown trout; note the straight, long pectoral fin.

A typical wild brown trout from a Catskill stream has well-formed, long, feathery, amber-colored pectoral fins; a golden/brown cast, often with bright red spots with white halos. At times even the adipose fin will have a red spot. The adipose fin and the base of the tail will be tinged red.

Fin erosion is so widespread that fisheries biologists across the country use poor fin development as a key to identifying stocked trout. Deformed pectoral or dorsal fins can compromise a trout's swimming ability and reduce its survival in the wild. The fins of hatchery trout can be degraded and reduced in size from abrasion or fin nipping. Hatchery trout are raised in unnatural densities generally in abrasive concrete raceways. Fin erosion can also occur because of malnutrition, bacterial infection (fin rot), poor water quality, excessive sunlight, and environmental contaminants.

It should be noted that some taxidermists have molded artificial soft plastic fins to replace all the damaged or deformed fins on hatchery trout that are brought in for mounting.

10. A hatchery-stocked trout; note the deformed pectoral fin.

Today's trout fishers are more concerned about the state of our wild trout fisheries than those of the past, and many become involved in programs aimed at increasing wild-trout populations through habitat improvement, special fishing regulations, and environmental disturbances that threaten fisheries resources.

6

FLIES THAT FLOAT

The proportions used are especially important. If each part is
not reasonably well-balanced with the others, the finished fly will be
unsatisfactory in one or more respects. Dry flies particularly must
be properly balanced to insure correct behavior on the surface.

J. EDSON LEONARD, *Flies* (1969)

The fly is the most important part of your equipment. It's not the rod, reel, line, or leader, it's the fly! The fly is what connects you to the fish. What does a good dry fly look like? It should be proportioned to the hook size—no part of the fly's makeup should be more exaggerated than the other. The fly should be neat and trim, and have no more turns of hackle than it needs to float properly. The hackle around the wings and the tail support the fly, in front and back; the wings should be upright and angled evenly so the fly can sit high on the surface film. It's important to tie dry flies that have a generally sparse appearance, with a finely tapered body, a matched pair of wings, and a limited amount of stiff quality dry-fly hackle.

11. A well-tied dry fly with a sparse appearance, matched wings, limited stiff hackle.

I once asked Elsie Darbee "How many turns of hackle do you make behind and in front of the wings?" I was a beginning fly-ti-er when I asked, and was hoping her answer would simplify and improve my fly-tying skills by giving me a definitive number. Elsie answered "There is no set amount of turns, it depends on the hack-le." As I gained experience I learned that what Elsie meant was that some hackle feathers are denser or stiffer than others and therefore require more or fewer turns, rather than a specific number of turns for every fly. Considerable importance should be placed on using the best possible dry flies and, in doing so, paying strict attention to the fly's profile, or silhouette, and balance. There are times when you can just look at a fly in your hand and know that the fly will catch fish–and that's what I remember thinking when I looked at Elsie Darbee's flies.

The wings of dry flies should be approximately as long as the length of the hook shank, from the eye to the bend of the hook, and they should be tied on halfway between the hook point and the eye of the hook. The length of the tail should also be from the eye of the hook to the bend, as with the wings. Lee Wulff, in his book *Lee Wulff on Flies*, provides good insight into the importance of the tail of the dry fly; as he explains, "The tail of the fly was most important since it would support the bend of the hook, where most of the weight is concentrated."

The body should be slim and slightly tapered, and the hackle 1 ½ times the gap of the hook or ¾ of the length of the upright wing. Even if you don't tie flies, you should be aware of a dry fly's proportions. I believe that one of the main reasons trout refuse to take a particular fly is because the fly is tied out of proportion and does not sit on the surface as a natural insect would.

It has been said that you can't tie a fly that will not catch a trout, but if you want to be more consistently successful on the stream under all conditions, you need to have properly tied dry flies. This cannot be stressed enough; you do not need to carry an abundance of different flies, but the flies you choose should be the best you can buy or tie. Learn about the proportions of a dry fly, and the shape and the perfection of the silhouette; recognize what a well-tied fly should look like. Everyone who takes his fly-fishing seriously should learn to tie his own flies, as it can add to your fishing pleasure. Purchasing a few books on tying that feature instructions would be helpful.

Although it is not difficult to learn how to tie flies, being able to tie a good fly takes practice and an understanding of what a good trout fly should look like. If you are tying, always use the best materials available.

Many professional fly-tiers do not like to use tanned furs for tying, preferring, if possible, natural fur with the oils still in the hide. They also favor naturally colored necks or capes, believing that dyed hackle used on dry flies is represented on the water as one solid color, whereas the tones on an undyed feather exhibit various naturally colored hues, especially in the dun shades.

Many flies are poorly tied, at times because of inferior materials, and are disproportioned by being over-hackled, bulky, and lacking the proper silhouette or shape to attract trout. Try to obtain a sample of the fly you would like to tie; don't fish with it, but use it as a model.

Fundamentally there are four shapes or profiles of floating flies that trout and trout fishers are familiar with. The most common is that of the mayfly, which typically appears on the stream's surface with upright wings in the shape of a sail. Its wings are held together while waiting for them to dry in order to fly from the stream to nearby vegetation. At times, perhaps to hasten the drying, mayflies will flex their wings into a V form while floating; similarly mayfly imitations are tied with upright wings that are divided to help make the fly balance, float better, and appear more natural on the surface film.

According to an article in the June 1, 2001 issue of the *Journal of the New York Entomological Society* titled "The Mayfly Fauna of New York State (Insecta: Ephemeroptera)" there are a total of 173 species of mayflies, representing fifteen families and forty-five genera. That's a lot of mayflies to imitate if you are looking to match the flies that are hatching!

A second profile trout are familiar with is that of the adult mayflies after they have mated and deposited their eggs. These are known as spinners or spent-wings, and trout encounter these flies throughout the fishing season. Many fall on the water's surface and float downstream, with their wings outstretched flat. Trout are well aware of the silhouettes of natural flies; and it's not unusual to fish a spent-wing fly pattern and have success, even when none are on the water.

A third shape or profile that trout recognize is that of the caddisfly, which is often referred to as "moth-like" in appearance. Caddis have antennae and no tails, with wings that are tent-like and folded over their body. Caddis dry flies are easier to tie than mayfly dries due to their shape, as caddisflies have a low profile and therefore do not need to be as balanced as their mayfly counterparts.

The fourth floating fly profile is the stonefly, which is slightly different from the caddisfly, in that the stonefly's wings are tied flat over their body.

Trout flies are made by hand, and well-tied flies are rarely produced in a hurry. Often, to make a greater profit, speed is applied to the process, and it becomes difficult to mass-produce quality flies, as this action generally turns out a product that is a far cry from what a good trout fly should look like. The way the fly is tied is crucial, and is more important than what the pattern is, or whether it matches the flies that are on the water. If your dry fly is tied properly and is not overdressed, it should float as if it were a natural, and drift along with the current, seemingly unattached.

Some flyfishers who have difficulty in catching a fish that is rising may resort to changing flies, believing they need a fly that better matches what the trout are feeding on. However, the problem may be a poorly tied fly. Poorly tied flies are most likely not going to fool the trout. The quality of the fly depends on the fly-tyer, the materials used, and the fly's proportions. There are different levels of fly-tying skills as well as the level of knowledge that goes into tying a fly properly. My fly-tying skills are average, but I am particular about how the flies are constructed. I do not take shortcuts, or vary the methods, but focus on quality materials and proper proportions.

There is a correlation between the wings, body, tail, and hackle; their individual proportions are important, because together they create a dry fly that is well-balanced and looks natural on the stream's surface.

Years ago someone once asked me how many fish could be caught on one fly. I didn't have a definitive answer at the time, but found an occasion in the diary dated May 10, 1984 that was related to the question: "Fished Willowemoc Creek 4:00-8:00, caught 5 wild B.T. (brown trout) 1 wild S.T. (brook trout) and 35 hatchery B.T. (total of 41) Caught 31 on one #14 Adams before it became unfishable (no body, or tail). Fished in Roscoe at bridge. Some Shad flies, female Hendricksons, few darkish mayflies on water but not really many fish rising. Most fish came up to the fly. Caught one fish with hook point & bend coming out the vent and snelled leader sticking out the mouth, the hook caught on the net and pulled the leader out of sight, so I pulled on the hook gently and the leader came out of the fish! (along with the hook of course) It passed through the fish." (I guess you could call this outpatient surgery.)

7

DRY-FLY REVELATIONS

*After playing with just about every conceivable type
of rod, line, leader and fly for twenty years, it is my conclusion
that expertness in casting and an understanding of the fish's
nature, are the two factors to success—The greatest mistake among
those who fish, it seems to me, is the neglect of attaining (casting)
efficiency while, at the same time, continually searching
the world for a fly which is infallible.*

PAUL YOUNG, *Making and Using the Dry Fly* (1933)

Through the years, I have rarely encountered anyone who did not believe in matching the hatch. Books, articles, and well-meaning flyfishers insisted that in order to be successful one must have the "right" fly—meaning in most cases, an accurate imitation of the fly on which the trout were feeding. This assumption caused many flyfishers to carry a diverse assortment of fly patterns, and ingrained a mindset of searching through their flies to find the right one after they had made a few casts with little success.

There are many anglers who believe that catching a trout on a fly is more complicated than it really is. Some are of the opinion that it is necessary to learn the Latin names of the aquatic insects to further differentiate between each one in order to replicate more accurately the exact fly on which the trout are feeding. And there are some who support this theory that are even confrontational with their viewpoint, though I have rarely seen a dry-fly imitation that actually resembles the natural insect it is supposed to typify. By placing too much emphasis on having the correct fly, one loses the ability to be innovative and hone skills that may already exist.

It is best to opt for a fly pattern that you have caught trout on previously: a fly pattern that you have confidence in, and that you know would be of interest to the trout–a well-tied fly, with good form or silhouette that is floating correctly and has the appearance of something the trout has seen before. Also, it is important to be patient and not change the fly pattern until after you have made a few good presentations that were refused.

Trout consume a multitude of aquatic insects, as well as crayfish, ants (especially those with wings), grasshoppers, mice, and even hemlock needles. Hemlock needles? I experienced this unusual revelation on a September day on a stretch of the Willowemoc that today flows past the Catskill Fly Fishing Center & Museum. I caught a wild brook trout of approximately 11 inches in length. I had seen hemlock needles on the stream's surface where the trout was rising, but was surprised when I caught the trout on an Adams and noticed it had a bulging stomach with a few hemlock needles in its mouth. Upon examining the stomach I discovered that the trout had been consuming the hemlock needles; the only resemblance between a hemlock needle and an aquatic insect is that both float on the surface of the water. And I know of no fly that imitates a hemlock needle!

I've always believed it was easier to catch trout on dry flies, and that if you were teaching someone to fish with flies it would be less challenging to begin with flies that float. Everything is visual: you observe the rise and cast a fly just upstream of the trout. The fact that the trout is rising indicates that the fish is feeding and is therefore hungry, and is looking for food. Although you can see the fly clearly, the trout is at a disadvantage because it's located in a different element (water) and gets a distorted view of the fly. This should enable you to fool the trout into thinking your fly is something it may have eaten before.

I've spent a lot of time thinking about the information revealed in my diaries, hoping that I might come up with a good answer as to why I have been so successful with a few flies that basically do not imitate any particular fly but do appear similar to several natural flies. How do I explain my ability to do so?

My immediate thought was that I fish more than most people. And, because I chose to live near the waters I fish, I don't need to spend a lot of time traveling to or from the stream or river. The more time you spend doing something the more successful you become. I remember the 10,000-hour rule in Malcolm Gladwell's popular non-fiction book *Outliers: The Story of Success*. Gladwell states that the key to becoming proficient at what you do in any skill is that you need to practice properly for 10,000 hours. The time spent should involve intensive practice that is done purposefully, rather than just tallying casual hours on the task. Presumably, 10,000 hours means 417 days' worth of hours, or three hours a day for 3,333 days –a little over nine years. Since I have been trout fishing for more than 60 years, I am certain I completed my 10,000 hours a long time ago.

Many years ago, angling writer Art Lee used to hassle me about the Adams dry fly, wishing that I would come up with a definitive answer for my success with the fly. I never had a definitive answer, but one person who may have was the late Lee Wulff. After Lee and Joan moved to the Catskills in 1979 and opened the Joan and Lee Wulff School of Fly Fishing, we fished together most every season on the Beaverkill, Willowemoc, Esopus, or Delaware. Lee analyzed my dry-fly fishing in his 1986 book, *Trout on a Fly*. He credited my "eyesight" and

"casting control" and stated that I drop the dry fly "at the very center of a rising trout's feeding lane, not, as most anglers do, inches or feet to one side or the other."

Lee Wulff's comments about dropping a dry fly at the center of a feeding lane reminded me of an incident that occurred while fishing with Art Lee. We were fishing Cairns Pool, the most popular pool on the lower Beaverkill. I once wrote in an article for *TROUT* Magazine that "the only days you can find no one fishing in Cairns is Christmas and New Year's," and then the next year there was a fisherman on New Year's Day.

I was fishing in the tail of Cairns Pool where the flow is at its slowest, and trout have ample time to look over your fly. Art was fishing upstream of me in similar water. I had caught a few fish on a size #14 Adams and then came across a trout that I had made several good presentations to, but it would not take. I wanted to rest the fish, and would have, but there were no other trout rising nearby. There was nothing wrong with my casting control; I had dropped the fly in the center of the trout's feeding lane more than once but was still coming up empty.

I was a little frustrated and began talking to myself. Art dropped down to where I was fishing, and started giving me some good-natured heckling about my inability to catch this particular fish, which continued working on the surface. While using some colorful language I made a cast that over-shot the fish and went a few inches beyond its feeding lane. The trout immediately took the Adams, and while playing the trout I puzzled, "I made a poor cast and the trout takes!"

After netting the fish I noticed that its left eye, the eye that had been facing me, was opaque; the fish was blind in that eye! But the right eye was fine. If I had not overcast the fish I probably would not have caught it.

12. Cairns Pool, the most popular pool on the Beaverkill.

8

PRESENTATION AND FISHING WITH CONFIDENCE

---

*There are two very essential requirements that the
angler must master for consistently successful dry-fly fishing.
These are: delicacy in presenting the fly, and the ability
to float that fly in a natural manner, the same as a natural fly
would float if carried along by the current.*

RAY BERGMAN, *Trout* (1938)

PRESENTATION

I agree with Ray Bergman, who describes the importance of presentation in successful dry-fly fishing. Presentation is the process of accurately and delicately "presenting," or placing, an artificial dry fly on the surface of the water in a realistic manner. Flyfishers who follow this school of thought and who do not believe that direct imitation of the fly or "matching the hatch" is necessary to be successful in catching fish are at times referred to as "Presentationists."

Presentationists tend to believe that artificial flies, even the best-tied imitations, are not similar in appearance to the natural fly floating on the water. Their perspective for success involves presenting the fly to the rising trout in the most natural manner possible, seemingly unattached to a leader.

An essential part of presentation is tippet size; the finer the tippet, the more natural the fly will look and float. My preference is to tie on a tippet that is one size finer than may be necessary. For example: a size #16 dry fly can be fished with 6X or 5X; however, if you use the 6X it will give the fly a better float.

The goal is to make the artificial fly have the appearance of a natural fly and float as a natural fly would, *on* the surface film, not *in* the surface film; and to make the presentation with such confidence that you expect that the trout is going to take the fly and are surprised if it doesn't. That's how I fish.

The first step of presentation is the position of the angler: where you stand in the river when you cast to a rising fish is extremely important. Your approach should be from downstream of the fish, which would be facing upstream. Wade out from shore if necessary, cautiously moving upstream until you can take a position opposite the trout that is rising. From this position you can get the best drag-free drift and the trout will see only the fly rather than your line or leader. I favor this position because my goal is to show the trout the best profile of my fly: a side view, rather than the fly approaching the fish "head first" or "tail first."

This position is also the best for setting the hook. There should be no slack in your cast; you will have better line control with short casts. If you position yourself to stand too far downstream of the rising fish, your cast upstream toward the rise may cause the leader to precede the fly on the drift toward the trout. The fish may spook or, if it attempts to take the fly, its nose or mouth may make contact with the leader and move the fly. This may result in a missed fish, or one that is poorly hooked. Similarly, if you are in the correct position but cast too far upstream ahead of the rise, your cast may cause the leader to precede the fly and spook the fish.

Furthermore, if you position yourself to stand too far upstream, ahead of the rising trout, you will actually be casting downstream toward it. The leader will not precede the fly, but if the trout "takes" the fly and you set the hook from that position, you may actually pull the fly out of the fish's mouth. To reiterate, the best position to fish from is to stand across from or opposite the rising trout.

Position will also influence whether or not your fly is affected by drag. "Drag" occurs when the current causes the mid-section of the fly line to develop a loop or belly that precedes the fly and results in dragging it along the water's surface unnaturally. If your position is correct, you can prevent drag by following the line with the rod tip after placing the fly on the water.

There are times when drag can be so slight that it goes unnoticed; this can occur because of the trout's position. It may be feeding in an area with cross currents, and the fly could be dragging so slightly that it is imperceptible to you, but not to the trout. Trout rarely take a fly that is dragging; it often causes them to spook or be on alert.

I have fished with a number of flyfishers who, after allowing the fly to land on the water, have a bad habit of immediately mending their line automatically, as if it was part of the cast. "Mending line" is gently picking up the excess line and placing it upstream of the fly to prevent drag.

However, if you are positioned correctly and make a good cast, mending the line should not be necessary. Mending is an action that often moves the fly on the water inadvertently–even at times pulling the fly below the surface. This activity alerts the trout to the fact that the fly is fraudulent. Some flyfishers continue mending line throughout the drift; a habit that may come from fishing from drift boats, and an attempt to extend the amount of time the fly is on the water. It's an unnecessary practice of wade flyfishers that is not part of a good presentation. Try to position yourself so that you don't need to mend the line.

If you desire to have a longer drift without drag, you can actually extend your line somewhat by "throwing slack" into your cast. After making the cast to the location you are seeking, stop the rod as you normally would, and then continue to move the rod upstream. Basically, what you are doing is placing extra line upstream, allowing for a longer drift.

It is important to be able to estimate the distance between you and the rising fish and cast accurately, placing your fly on a course that puts it directly on a path to float in the center of the trout's feed lane. The fly should be within inches of where the trout is rising. If you are having difficulty in gauging the distance, you can false cast a couple of times behind the trout: this will help you to estimate the distance between you and the fish.

There are special instances when you can alter your cast in order to give the fly a longer drift on the surface, such as when the depth of the water prevents you from wading out any further, or if you are fishing a fast run. You can extend your cast as follows: after you've released the line at the end of your cast, push the rod upstream, to place as much extra line behind the fly as possible. This will enable the fly to have a longer, drag-free float.

The fly alone should be all that the trout sees: no leader, no line, just the fly. If you cast beyond the rise you may "line" the trout (meaning the line may go over the trout ahead of the fly) and cause the fish to become wary. If you cast too short the fish may see the fly drag, and again be placed on alert. It may continue to rise but sense that something is not quite right and may not take your next cast even though it is in the feed lane.

If your first cast was accurate and the trout did not take, hold the line in your left hand to maintain the same amount of line so that the next cast will go exactly where the first went. This is an advantage of fishing with a fly rod. Being able to judge the distance between you and the fish is not always easy but is a skill that time spent practicing will improve.

Always respect a trout's space. If the trout does not take your fly, or if you make a poor cast, wait until the line drifts out of the trout's area before picking up as much of the line off the water as possible, raising the rod and lifting the rest into the air quietly with the least disturbance. Don't rip or pluck the line and the fly off the water as soon as it passes the trout's location. If you know you have made a

13. Ed "on point" leaning forward to fully concentrate on a rising fish.

good presentation three or four times and the trout has ignored the fly, rest the fish and move to another.

Accuracy is a very important step in presentation. Too many false casts may possibly spook the fish. In addition, the more casts you make to a rising trout, the more apt you are to put the fish down by making a poor cast or causing some other type of disturbance that spooks the trout–even though it may continue to rise, it may not take an artificial fly.

I have fished many times with Phil Chase, of Port Jervis, who often would remark, "Eddie is on point!" meaning that I was concentrating on a particular fish that was rising so much so that I would lean forward and cast intently, with very few false casts in between.

Your cast should be synchronized with the timing of the trout as it takes naturals from the surface. Trout often fall into a rhythm during a hatch and timing your cast can be an important part of your presentation. This will help to enable your fly and the trout to meet on that "collision course." If done correctly this action makes it more difficult for the trout not to take the fly, especially during an abundant hatch.

Most trout take up a position to feed when a hatch is occurring on the surface, especially brown trout, and they do not move very far from their position. Rainbow trout, however, often cruise an area and surface at different places, especially on the Delaware. This of course can change, depending on the number of flies riding on the surface, the water temperature, the trout's anxiety, and wariness. The better your presentation, the more enticing your fly will be to the trout.

There are times when feeding lanes are defined by small currents, patches of foam, or tiny bits of flotsam; this makes your target more evident, making it easier to catch fish. I was fishing on the Esopus late in the year, where a decent-sized tributary entered the mainstream. I watched Blue-Wing Olive-type flies floating in the foam and being taken; the foam prevented the flies from leaving the water and the trout took advantage of the situation. In order to catch fish, it was necessary to cast in a certain spot above where the trout were rising and allow the fly to be gathered in the foam and brought down to the feeding trout. This observation resulted in a very successful fishing trip.

An example of good presentation occurred one day when I was fishing with Joan and Lee Wulff along Sherwood's Flats on the Willowemoc Creek "No Kill" area. Lee was fishing downstream from where I was, and Joan upstream. We were spaced a decent distance from one another, not near enough to speak without talking loudly, but close enough that we could see how well the other was doing.

There was a good hatch, and trout were working up and down the pool. We all had good numbers of fish rising steadily in front of our position. The Wulffs had not fished the Willowemoc before, and I was anxious for them to like the river. We began catching trout immediately; at times each of us had a fish on, all at the same time. I had no idea what Lee or Joan were fishing with, but I was using an Adams.

This type of action continued for about an hour. Joan and I were still catching fish, but I noticed that Lee was not doing as well as when we first arrived. He seemed to be spending more time changing flies, though he still caught a trout every once in a while. At one point I reeled up and waded down to where Lee was fishing to see if I could be helpful and suggest a different fly.

Not wanting to appear as though I was trying to tell Lee Wulff how to fish, I chose my words carefully and asked him if he would like to try my spot as there seemed to be more fish there. He declined and said there were just as many rising where he was, but he wasn't catching as many as before because he was "trying to see what fly they wouldn't take." I was taken aback and wondered if my skill level would ever reach the point where I would try to see what the trout wouldn't take!

I often thought that what Lee was accomplishing was the result of his experience and being such a skilled presentationist, that he was able to present a fly to a trout in a manner that the fish could not refuse, no matter what the pattern.

Many years ago, on the Delaware River, I stood alongside a friend who was a seasoned angler and had a large rainbow rising steadily in front of him. The trout was so close that we could observe its every move. I would estimate its size to be close to twenty inches. My friend tied on a dry fly, made a few casts, then changed to a different pattern. He did this three or four times and not once did he put the fly and the trout together. The fly went too far to the right because he over-cast, then too far to the left, because he under-cast.

The trout was holding its position; it would rise, take a fly, and drop back below the surface and wait for the next floater. There was no attempt on the part of my friend to time the rise. At times his fly would reach the trout just after the fish had taken a natural and was easing back below the surface.

It was painful to watch, as this trout was feeding steadily and should have been caught, but the angler was too focused on having the right fly, stating "well he doesn't want that one," and would tie on another, never really giving the trout a chance to take the fly. I believe the rainbow would have taken anything if the fly had been properly presented. Had my friend concentrated on working to present the fly properly he may well have had success in catching the fish.

FISHING WITH CONFIDENCE

Some flyfishers cast their dry-fly imitations and *hope* that the trout is going to take their fly. They tend to put their faith in the fly pattern, believing that the trout may not take their fly if it is not a good imitation of the fly that is hatching. However, the real problem may be in their presentation of the fly rather than the fly itself.

When a trout is rising, try to make your first cast the best and *expect* the trout to take the fly on that cast. I always expect the trout to take the fly on the first cast, and am surprised if it doesn't.

If you use flies that are well-tied, no matter what the pattern, and are careful in your presentation of that fly, placing it in the trout's feeding lane and being aware of the timing of your cast, you should have confidence that the trout will take the fly. Fishing with confidence is a definite advantage, and I believe this is one of the reasons for my success in fishing.

I remember reading about fishing with confidence in Al McClane's book, *The Practical Fly Fisherman*. McClane relates that he was fishing the Neversink with his friend Charles Ritz, the famed hotelier, known for his fly-casting and fly-fishing abilities. The river was more crowded than usual, and no one was catching fish; finally, Ritz hooked into a large brown trout that made quite a commotion before he netted it. An angler fishing downstream of Ritz asked him what fly he was using, and he replied "a Coachman". Al related the results of that reply:

> *"In a moment the word that binds all anglers sounded like drums along the Mohawk–everybody was passing the information on. There was a clicking of fly boxes and some streamside swapping, and I know for a fact that two people fishing just below me caught trout soon afterward."*

Al reeled up and went over to Ritz and watched him land his third fish, and in the process, he noticed that Ritz was using a Bivisible, not a Coachman:

> *"We didn't speak for several minutes, until one angler let out a whoop of victory; then Charley remarked quite casually, 'Everybody has faith in the Coachman.'"*

9

DRY-FLY TACTICS
AND PLOYS

*The difference between good casters and
mediocre ones lies in little details, and in the disciplines
needed to maintain control over the line.*

JOAN SALVATO WULFF, *Joan Wulff's Fly Fishing* (2024)

I t is remarkable that we are able to fashion an artificial dry fly with bits of feathers and snips of fur tied with gossamer thread onto a hook made of steel, and then float the object in an attempt to deceive a trout into believing it is something edible that the trout has seen before. The best part is, that we get to watch everything, and see how it plays out.

Although I have stated that for years I have used and depended on a minimal number of dry-fly patterns, my success with the dry fly hinges on certain tactics and several disciplines that I adhere to.

There are times when no trout are rising, and you wish to fish with dry flies. I find that it is best to fish the fast water with some depth near the head of the pool or between pools. I use a fly that is easy to see and floats well, such as an Elk-Hair Caddis or a Royal Wulff. A fly that can be seen as soon as it lands in fast water provides an advantage, because the take will be unexpected. Quick reflexes and proficient eye-hand coordination are needed to set the hook.

Trout inhabiting fast water are accustomed to making speedy decisions. They must make up their minds quickly or food goes floating by. In fast water I generally use a larger fly and tippet size to make the fly more visible.

If you are prospecting and not having much success, change flies to one with a different shape, from an upright-wing dry fly to a caddis imitation, or vice versa, rather than changing patterns to just another mayfly or caddisfly. I find that deer-hair body flies are good to prospect with as they also float well in fast water; and their larger size and shape will attract the trout's attention.

After catching a few fish, the dry fly may become a little disheveled and may not float as well as when it was first tied on. This may coincide with the action slowing down. And if the fly is not floating well, it may be necessary to change flies. I'll often tie on a fresh fly of the same pattern, and as a rule use floatant before making the first cast, whenever flies are changed.

14. Flying Caddis Fly, a deer-hair bodied fly that floats well in fast water.

If trout are rising, I generally fish with an Adams, regardless of which species of flies are hatching, unless there is a hatch of midges. I match the size of the fly to that which is hatching and likewise the tippet to the size of the hook. During a trout's lifetime, they see a great many different fly hatches, with flies of various sizes in numerous hues, shades, and colors, and will take an artificial fly that resembles something familiar. A fly like the Adams, dressed properly, with an overall blue-gray color, as are many natural mayflies, can take trout even during a hatch of Sulphurs, for example. It's not that trout aren't concentrated at times on one particular fly that's hatching, but I believe a well-tied fly floating high on the surface in the path of a rising trout has a good chance of being accepted because its form or shape and color is something the trout has seen before.

Most of the time when I have tried a different dry-fly pattern, it was during a period of no surface activity and I was prospecting, trying to bring up fish. There have also been times when I just wanted to try something different to see if it would work.

When you are not actually casting to a rising trout, your eyes should be searching for rises. It is easier to cast to a trout that is feeding than to prospect the water and try to entice a trout to take the fly. Additionally, when you are playing a fish, your eyes should be looking for the next trout to cast to.

When prospecting I often fish the fast water or head of a pool first and take advantage of the flow until nearly dark, then drop down and fish the slower water where larger trout are more apt to be. Trout in the fast water are easier to catch because the fish has learned to take the food quickly, so it doesn't pass by in the current. You may need to strike more quickly, and a larger fly with a slightly heavier tippet can be more helpful in preventing you from breaking off.

It is important to remember that trout in slow or flat water are more difficult to catch than trout in fast water. In slow water the fish have more time to look over your fly as it moves slowly through the pool. Flies used in slower water should also be smaller, sparser, and tied on a finer tippet.

If you are fishing in the early evening and notice a good trout working in the tail of the pool you might want to give that fish a look at your fly. But if it doesn't take your fly on the first couple of casts, move on and wait until the light starts fading, and then give the fish another try. Remember that as it becomes darker, it's easier to deceive the trout.

You can leave a stream too early, especially larger streams or rivers. Many mayflies and caddisflies hatch after dark; oftentimes a spinner fall may occur when you can no longer see your fly and have decided to leave. I have never read much about flies hatching after dark but have often witnessed the water being covered with flies while crossing a river and shining a flashlight, and have had many hit the windshield while driving along the stream after dark.

Trout tend to feed more at this time of day, especially larger trout. As the evening progresses, trout become a little more careless, and will take a fly on a slightly heavier tippet. At twilight, I tend to increase the tippet size to 4X, from 5X or 6X, because there is a chance I'll be striking a rise in the dark, or near dark, and I may need a slightly stronger tippet. Another rationale is to lessen the chance of the fly breaking off a finer tippet and having to tie on a new fly in the dark. One need not see the fly to catch trout under these conditions; if you can see the rise, cast ahead of it and strike when you see the rise again, knowing your fly should be in that general area. Try this approach and you may be surprised at how successful it can be. I have fished on numerous occasions when it made the difference between catching trout and not catching trout.

Fishing with a white line is helpful under these conditions, as it is easier to see and tell where your fly might be. When you hear and see a surface disturbance you should set the hook: more often than not you will have hooked the fish. I've had good success with an Adams at these times, perhaps the fly's dark appearance may be easier for the trout to see against the fading light than a light-colored fly.

Some anglers believe that brown trout are more selective than rainbows, though I have never found this to be true. On large rivers rainbows require more precise presentation than browns, because they often move while they are rising, whereas browns tend to stay in one place and are easier to zero in on. On the Delaware I have seen rainbows begin to rise below where I'm standing and work their way upstream continuing to rise. Many times I have moved with the fish and concentrated on dropping the fly just ahead of them.

If trout are not rising, I rarely stay in one place very long, depending on how much time is left in the day and where I am located. I do like to move around and tend to go back and forth between fast water and pools looking for rises. Even when I'm playing a fish, my eyes are always alert, watching for rises and the next trout I should be casting to. I fish aggressively. This doesn't mean I'm not having fun, it means I'm having *more* fun.

Remember that in high water one can get away with using larger flies; but as levels drop and stream velocity slows, it's important to choose smaller and more natural-looking flies, as the fish has more time to look over the fly in slower water.

After I make a cast, if the fly is sitting upright and riding on the surface film well, I may "walk the dog," or wade slowly downstream with the fly to get a longer than usual float. The longer the fly is on the water the greater the chance for the trout to take the fly. I've done this many times when I know I'm fishing good water, such as on the Delaware or lower East and West Branches, especially if I am prospecting and nothing is feeding on the surface. My eyes are on the fly but I also "sneak-peek" and look for rises.

If a trout comes up and looks at the fly but does not take, the unwritten rule is that you drop a hook size but stay with the same pattern. There are also times when a trout may attempt to take your fly, but you were a little late, or early, or too fast, or too slow in setting the hook and missed the fish. A good rule to follow is to rest the trout for a few minutes, then try the same fly a size smaller, as long as you are sure the fish didn't feel the hook. If the trout did feel the hook, rest the fish and try for it later.

If you are not having success with regard to your presentation, there are a number of considerations to be aware of rather than your choice of fly, such as whether your casting accuracy needs improving, or if your approach to a rising trout is as discreet as it could be. Other things to consider are whether the length of the tippet has become too short from tying on a number of flies, or if the tippet size is too large for the fly you're using, or if the fly is dragging in the surface before it reaches the fish.

Another tactic used when the trout takes your offering, but you didn't set the hook and failed to catch the fish, is to change to a different pattern and try with a totally different fly.

Most trout adopt a place to feed when a hatch is on the surface. This of course can change depending on the number of flies riding the surface, water temperature, the fish's anxiety, and perhaps wariness. The better you make your presentation, the harder it will be for the trout not to take your fly.

When fishing over rising trout, casting accuracy is important, especially when a trout will not move out of its feeding lane. Try not to mend line when fishing a dry fly; this not only can move the fly, which will put the trout on alert, but it also adds moisture to the fly, making it sit lower in the surface film.

There are occasions when the trout appear to be trying to take every fly that floats by. Some actually develop a rhythm while feeding on the surface, and you can "time" the fish's rise. In these instances it is best to shorten the drift. By false casting, you can wait until the trout is expected to come up to the surface. Concentrate on dropping the fly close to where the fish is rising. Make sure your timing in dropping the fly coincides with when you expect the trout to rise.

Trout that are rising are easier to catch because you can observe how they react to your fly and see them take the fly. You can follow your fly and anticipate where and when the fish will take it, an advantage that you don't have when prospecting or fishing the water.

If you lose a fish that was on the end of your line, or if you suddenly begin to miss trout on the take, it's important to check the hook point on the fly, as it may have become bent or even broken off.

If you notice a wind knot, take the time to replace the section where the knot occurred. A wind knot creates a weak spot in your leader.

After catching a large fish, it's a good idea to retie your fly, as large trout have sharp teeth that can fray the tippet, and their size and weight can also stretch the tippet, making it weaker. Large fish like to go under or between rocks, which can also fray and weaken the tippet.

1 0

THE ADAMS DRY FLY

The best tied pattern is the one that gives the impression of being a wide range of flies, sufficiently vague as to imitate none in particular exactly but suggestive of a great many. Even then there is no "right" fly unless it is presented properly and fished correctly.

JOHN ROBERTS, *To Rise a Trout* (1988)

At the top of my list of successful dry flies is the Adams, and the fly fits perfectly into John Roberts' description. I believe that the Adams works exceptionally well because of the blending of the hackle. The red/brown hackle mixed with grizzly gives the fly a multi-colored natural appearance, not a solid one, resulting in an optical imprecise image that is reminiscent of a number of natural mayflies. Artist, fly-tyer, and angling author John Atherton also favored blending hackles, believing they were more lifelike than solid color hackles.

Many years ago, most likely in the 1980s, I was asked by Art Lee how I was able to catch so many trout on a fly like the Adams that didn't really match any particular fly hatch. At the time, I most likely just shrugged and said I didn't know. I had never really given much

15. The Adams does not imitate any specific fly, but is similar in color to several blue/gray mayfly species.

thought as to why, I just continued to use the fly if trout were rising. But having recently put more serious thought to the question, I realized that the Adams does imitate a number of hatches: Hendrickson, Isonychia, and Blue-Winged Olive.

The Adams has a general blue-gray appearance that is prevalent in many mayfly hatches, and although the Adams does not directly imitate any specific hatches the fly is similar to several of the many blue/gray mayflies that ride the surface.

When cast among Hendricksons riding the water, in late April or early May, a size #14 Adams blends in nicely with the naturals. The same is true with the slate-colored Isonychia, a very popular mayfly hatch that occurs in the Catskills as early as May and June and as late as August and September. The Adams is also a look-alike of the abundant Blue-Winged Olive hatches that occur throughout the fishing season and into November on our rivers and streams, from size #14 through #18.

I remember a situation when the Lower Beaverkill was covered with Hendricksons downstream of Cooks Falls. I was fishing with a #14 Adams and it was difficult to determine which fly was mine. I wasn't sure if the trout were taking my fly or not. Despite the prolific hatch and numbers of rises, I had not caught anything; I believed that some fish were taking my fly but it was challenging trying to pick out the Adams from the natural flies on the water amid so many rises. I decided to tie on a Royal Wulff, as its white wings provided a good contrast from the slate-colored Hendricksons. It was a good decision, which resulted in my catching several on the Royal Wulff.

When I began using the Adams I first tied the pattern as a spent wing. It was about the same time that I started fishing the Delaware River from Callicoon to Hancock, in 1963-64.

One evening I waded out in the flow and shined my flashlight on the surface to see what was causing the feeding activity. I discovered that the water was covered with spent mayflies; their outstretched wings provided a silhouette that could be easily duplicated. At the time the Adams spent-wing was the only spent fly pattern that I knew of and I tied a few size #14s; on my next trip to the big river I was successful in catching a couple of late-feeding rainbows.

Being a dark fly, the Adams shows up well in contrast to the brighter evening sky, and trout looking up to the surface may see its shape better than that of a light-colored fly. The spent Adams, with its grizzly hackle-tip wings lying flat on the surface made a noticeably dark silhouette against the slowly fading light of the sky.

At times the fly could no longer be seen, but the use of a white floating line gave an indication of the fly's approximate location. If a rise or disturbance on the surface occurred, it was time to set the hook.

The Adams tied with upright wings also appeared so natural on the water that it became my fly of choice every time trout were rising on the surface, day or evening. It became so effective that I began to tie and carry a supply of Adams from #12 to #20 every season. I believe the fly works well because the Adams represents something familiar that the trout has seen before.

According to Harold H. Smedley's book, *Fly Patterns and Their Origins*, the Adams was first tied by Leonard Halladay, of Mayfield, Michigan, in about 1922. The popular fly pattern was named after Charles F. Adams, an attorney from Lorain, Ohio. Adams was an avid trout fisherman who fished the Boardman, a well-known Michigan trout stream.

In the early printings of *Fly Patterns and Their Origins,* Smedley did not include a photo of the Adams nor a pattern on how to tie the fly. However, in the fourth edition, copyrighted in 1950, he included photos of the Adams and gave the pattern provided by Leonard Halladay. The photo of the wings shows a pair of grizzly hackle tips tied half-spent and leaning forward at an unusual angle. The fly's appearance is quite different from the Adams of today, and was tied as follows:

LEONARD HALLADAY'S ADAMS

BODY: gray wool yarn.
TAIL: two strands from a golden pheasant neck feather.
HACKLE: mixed, from neck feathers of Barred Plymouth Rock rooster, and Rhode Island Red roosters.
WINGS: narrow neck feathers of Barred Plymouth Rock rooster, tied "advanced" forward and in a semi-spent manner.

As is stated above, the wings were tied leaning forward of the hackle on a 45-degree angle and "semi-spent."

The Adams also appeared in Paul Young's *Making and Using the Dry Fly* (1933). In Young's book, the fly is listed in a section titled "Spent-Winged Dry Flies," in which he gives instructions on how to tie a Spent-Winged Adams. Young writes that the Adams is a new fly that originated in Michigan. His pattern is as follows:

PAUL YOUNG'S ADAMS

TAIL: 5-6 fibers Golden Pheasant neck
BODY: Gray yarn
WINGS: pair of Plymouth Rock rooster hackle tips tied spent
HACKLE: one brown and one grizzly (Plymouth Rock)

While Young's alteration is minute, and involved a slight change of the grizzly hackle tips, the Adams went from 'semi-spent' wings to upright and divided wings when Catskill fly-tyers tied a new image of the classic fly created by Leonard Halladay, as described below by Tom Deschaine:

> As the fly continued to grow in popularity its reputation was spreading further and further from its point of origin. Sometime in the late 20s or very early 30s the Catskill tiers influenced the next modifications: the wings were pulled back from the 'advanced' position and they went from 'semi-spent' to upright and divided. The body was well trimmed and tapered in typical Catskill style.

"The Adams: History Revisited," (www.michigandryflies.net)

Over the years the Adams has been modified many times. In *Flies*, Leonard lists two Adams dry-fly patterns: a male and a female. Both patterns are tied spent-wing with grizzly hackle tips, both have brown and grizzly hackle, and brown and grizzly mixed hackle tails. However, while they are similarly tied with a gray muskrat-dubbed body, the female has a yellow chenille egg sac. I've never tied or fished with the female Adams, but would bet that it would catch trout.

Three years later, in A. J. McClane's *The Practical Fly Fisherman*, he made reference to an Adams Quill dry fly, stating: "It is generally accepted that an angler can get along with four or five different fly patterns and catch trout anywhere. You can do a very competent job with an Adams Quill, a Light Cahill, Brown Bivisible and a Royal Coachman (hair wing), for instance, provided the fly behaves like an insect after you throw it on the water."

Lee Wulff let his thoughts be known about the Adams in *Lee Wulff on Flies*. "For the natural dry fly, I'd choose the Adams. It looks like an imitation of so many natural insects that I feel it's invaluable. The Adams is mottled, has semi-translucent wings and a body of medium color density. I believe it is the buggiest-looking dry fly of all. . ."

In 1992, Eric Leiser published *The Dettes: A Catskill Legend*, a book devoted to Walt and Winnie Dette and their daughter Mary Dette Clark. One of the many dry flies featured in the text is the Delaware Adams, a pattern Walt designed for Art Lee.

THE DELAWARE ADAMS

THREAD: White
WINGS: Grizzly hackle tips
BODY: Medium olive wool palmered with Grizzly hackle
HACKLE: Grizzly & Brown
TAIL: Grizzly & Brown

Perhaps the most popular variation of the Adams dry fly is the Parachute Adams, which I have never tied or used; actually, I have only ever tied the Adams in the standard pattern, either with spent wings or with the wings upright.

My success with the Adams dry fly is the result of being very particular about how it is tied, especially its proportions and the materials used. I tie my dry flies in the "Catskill Style," with an overall sparse appearance and a finely tapered body, matched divided wings, and sparse, stiff glossy hackle, and use well-shaped grizzly hackle tips. The grizzly wings are the most important feature of the fly and should have good shape or form and hold that shape when they are tied to the hook shank. For many years I have raised grizzly roosters for the sole purpose of supplying grizzly hackle and hackle tips for tying the Adams. At times, I pick up a rooster and snip off the ends of saddle feathers when they are at their best, well-shaped, fairly rigid, and less absorbent of water.

Unfortunately, modern genetics have changed the capes and saddle hackles of roosters that are selectively bred for fly-tying; these feathers have evolved to where they are generally too narrow and are useless for winged flies that require hackle tips. By the time you stroke the feather to achieve a hackle-tip wing there is nothing left, there is no shape or conformation. Today, the best wing tips are found on the saddle hackles of bantam grizzly roosters; the barring on bantams is narrower and is more desirable.

I tip my hat to Leonard Halladay for creating such a wonderful dry fly. I could not have chosen any other dry fly that would have been as successful as the Adams.

11

MIDGE FISHING

It's hard to believe that even a small trout would spend
its energy gathering microscopic insects that are so small hundreds
would be needed to fill a tablespoon, yet some of the biggest
fish rise freely on these occasions.

A.J. McCLANE, *The Compleat McClane* (1988)

Midge is the common term for insects of the order Diptera—true
flies. They can be recognized by their having only one pair of
wings instead of two as do mayflies, caddisflies, and stoneflies.

Scientists tell us that the midge larva, of the family Chironomidae,
can be found in super abundance in fresh water, and that they are very
important to the diet of young-of-the-year trout. What is noteworthy is
that trout of all sizes feed on these tiny midges, and one has to wonder
why insects so small would appeal to adult trout. My thought would
be that they do so out of habit, or instinct.

Midges are a primary trout food supply in both cold and warm
weather. They may hatch throughout the fishing season during every
month of the year, and yet midge fishing may be the least practiced

form of fly-fishing. Most likely this is because the fly imitations of midges are so small they often cannot be seen by many flyfishers. I have heard this criticism countless times, and have formed the opinion that most anglers do not feel comfortable fishing with a fly they cannot see. And yet, fishing with midges on a size #22 hook with 7X or 8X tippet, on a soft seven- or eight-foot fly rod, is challenging and enjoyable.

I have seen trout feeding on midges for days, even in the coldest weather. My diary reveals that on opening day of the trout season, on April 1, 1970, the water temperature of the Willowemoc Creek 8:00 a.m. was 33 degrees Fahrenheit at Livingston Manor, one degree above freezing, and yet an hour or two later trout were rising to midges. At the time I was a Census Agent, and recorded that trout fishing was good in the "No Kill" area, and that runoff had not started and the water was particularly clear. Melting snow water tends to discolor the river's flow, causing some anglers to believe that it is not a good time to fish for trout. The following year (1971) even before opening day, on several sunny days in February and March when the air temperatures were around freezing, there were dozens of trout in a long flat pool of the lower Willowemoc taking midges off the surface. Actually, as is often the case when midges are hatching, the flies were hardly visible but trout could be seen slowly rising, unhurriedly, with barely a disturbance to the water. The rise was hardly apparent and disturbed the water surface little more than a large raindrop. Occasionally, I would see a dorsal fin and tail tip as a trout broke the stream's surface. Midge feeding activity is not splashy, but is quiet, slow, and deliberate.

My diaries reveal that in the "No Kill" portions of the Beaverkill and Willowemoc they can even be on the water in the blustery month of November when water temperatures are in the high 30s to the low 40s. However, these appearances are more apt to occur on sunny days, when air temperatures are at least 32 degrees Fahrenheit.

When I first began fly-fishing, I ignored fishing for trout that were midging or feeding on flies that were difficult to see. I had emptied my fly box trying all of the smallest flies I carried, most likely of size #18; nothing I had was of interest, but the trout continued rising, making the event more frustrating.

It became apparent that in order to catch trout that were feeding on midges, it was necessary to use flies tied on size #22 hooks or smaller, though I was skeptical that fish could even be caught on flies that size.

I recalled reading that when trout in England were feeding off the surface on midges the rise form was called "smutting," and that midge flies were labeled "fisherman's curses"—a connotation I attributed to mean that fishing with midges was very challenging.

I didn't ignore the possibility of fishing with size #22 hooks for very long. During one of my first summers fishing the lower Beaverkill I became attracted to the water at Wagon Tracks, below Cairns Pool. Wagon Tracks is one of those rare pools that can be fished equally as well from either side, and it seemed as though every time I visited the pool, there were trout midging. Some trout were of good size and, instead of reeling up and going elsewhere, I realized it was time to try fishing with 7X and miniscule dry flies.

At first I was tempted to tie up twelve-foot leaders with 7X tippets, but decided to continue using a nine-foot leader instead. My rationale was that it would be even more difficult to find a size #22 fly at the end of a twelve-foot leader than it would a nine. Though my experience was limited, I did notice that when trout were rising to midges they were not particularly spooky. They seemed focused on the minute fly, and perhaps the fish needed to concentrate to see the flies because of their small size. It was possible to wade fairly close to the trout that were rising to midges. I tied a couple of different patterns on a size #22 hook and caught a few fish, which gave me confidence.

That was a long time ago, and since then I've grown to appreciate midge fishing. I have had success on days when there was no other trout feeding activity except for midges. I like the extra challenge of catching trout on flies that are hardly visible, and on leaders as fine as a hair from a horse's mane.

When trout are rising to midges, they move very little after taking up a position in the water column to intercept the flies that are hatching; perhaps this is because the hatches are so abundant they don't need to move. Success at these times hinges on casting accuracy: placing the fly on a collision course with the trout is a must. Even an inch or two to the left or right can be rejected. It would be easy to misinterpret this as a refusal and change flies, but it may just be that the fly is not exactly in front of the trout.

I believe that it was fishing with midges that taught me how to be more successful overall at dry-fly fishing. Midge fishing is a bit more technical in the sense that things need to be more exact, such as presentation and casting accuracy, as well as timing, and size of the fly.

There are some trout, perhaps more eager, which move about the pool feeding on midges here and there and at times work their way past you. This maneuver requires trying to guess where the fish is going to rise next, and casting your fly where you estimate that rise will be, which can be challenging.

As I had learned many years ago on that early midge-fishing experience, when trout are engaged in feeding on midges they become so focused that wading within a reasonable distance of them is possible. With caution one can get close to the fish, at times even close enough to observe the fish just below the surface, gently finning as if in slow motion, and fixated on the tiny flies above. The rise form is quiet and, as I had first observed in that 1971 diary entry, often portrays a trout's head followed by the tip of its tail. The rise can be smooth and silent. One should focus on individual trout that are rising, and continue casting just ahead of the fish. Concentrate on casting to the rises rather than prospecting and fishing the water.

The life cycle of Diptera is similar to that of caddisflies in that the first three stages, egg, larva, and pupa, are spent underwater. Trout are said to feed on both the legless and worm-like midge larvae and pupae more than they do the adult midge, which looks like a mosquito. Larvae measure less than 1/4 inch, with the most common colors being red, green, black, and brown. The larvae travel to the surface and become the pupal stage. The pupae hang vertically in the water with their heads up, their tails down, and their gills in the surface film. Trout can take the larvae at the surface, as well as the drifting pupae; feeding is evident even in the underwater stages. The fly pattern is not as important as the size. A size #22 hook works best, along with 7X or 8X tippet if flows are low.

It is best to cast at right angles to the trout that are rising so that only the fly, not the leader, enters the trout's feeding lane. Although seeing your fly is certainly an advantage, one can also catch trout without seeing the fly if you know where your fly should be. After making a cast, follow the line, knowing your fly is about nine feet from the end of the line (if you are using a nine-foot leader). If you see a rise where you believe the fly should be, raise the rod and tighten the line. It's not necessary to move the rod too much, as you are fishing with 7X. When trout rise to a midge it's usually very deliberate, because the fly is so small, and hooking the fish is not difficult.

Casting accuracy is important, along with line control and positioning your cast close to where the trout is rising. Your mindset should be on timing and accuracy. You can time the trout by false casting. The goal is to put the fly and the fish together on a collision course, and the further you cast upstream of the fish, the harder it is to achieve this. If you can make your artificial midge arrive in front of the fish at the moment the trout is rising to the surface, the trout will take it. If your midge is not taken and reaches the end of its drift, and the line is ready to be lifted for the next cast, it should be taken off the water quietly. Playing trout on a 7X tippet is fun, no matter how small the fish is. It is helpful to hold the fish in a net when removing the tiny hook.

Remembering that a key element of fishing with midges is not the fly pattern, but rather the size of the fly; this is often dictated by the size of the hackle. The length of the hackle should be one- and one-half times the gap of the hook, no larger. Midge imitations do well without wings: simply a hackle, body, and tail will suffice if the fly's proportions are correct. The hackle determines how high the fly will sit on the water, which is extremely important. Many flyfishers do not do well with midges primarily because they tie, or buy, #22 flies with hackle that is too large. Most of the midge flies I see in shops, catalogs, and flyfishers' fly boxes are tied with over-sized hackle, with feathers that would fit a #20 or #18 hook, and because of this their #22 flies appear too large. A size #22 hackle is extremely small, and is generally found at the very top of a rooster's cape.

My favorite midge pattern, and one I am never without, is the Pheasant-Tail Midge. The fly is said to have been created by an English fly-fisherman named Payne Collier in or about 1901. While there appear to be a few variations of the fly pattern, the one that I use has no wings. The tail is made from two fiber tips from the center tail feather of a cock pheasant; which after tying on the tail are then wound forward for the body. The hackle is natural light blue or honey dun–naturally colored rather than dyed.

I do tie and at times use other midge fly patterns besides the Pheasant-Tail Midge including the Speckled Midge, Dun Midge, and Badger Quill, all on size #22 hooks:

16. My favorite midge pattern is the Pheasant-Tail Midge.

As is my habit when fishing with dry flies, if I have made a few good presentations to a trout with the fly floating high and upright and the trout has not exhibited any interest, and I think it should have, I may rest the fish by casting to another that is rising nearby. My intention is to return to the first fish after a few casts elsewhere. I don't like to spend too much time on one fish. There could be a reason the trout ignored a good presentation: there could have been unseen drag, or the trout may have been caught a short time earlier and is a little wary.

Trout can rise to midges at Hazel Bridge Pool, on the lower Willowemoc Creek, practically every month of the year. This pool is one of the most favored on the Willowemoc "No Kill" stretch, where all trout must be returned to the water unharmed. This is public water and it gets a great deal of fishing pressure. It can be fished year round, although there are a couple of months when it can be frozen over.

Like Cairns on the Beaverkill, the pool is also a gathering place of flyfishers and while most will be fishing, others watch from the bridge overlooking the pool, offering advice on what flies to use and pointing out rises to those in the water. If trout aren't rising to midges at Hazel Bridge Pool, they aren't rising anywhere on the Willowemoc.

The vast majority of the trout found in Hazel Bridge Pool are stocked brown-trout yearlings of about eight to nine inches; although there are a good number of holdovers and wild browns that in some years may average 12 to 14 inches, and it is not unusual to catch trout in the 15-inch-plus range. It's difficult to determine how many times an individual trout may have been caught repeatedly, and because of this, some of the fish can be challenging to catch.

Even though I tend to shy away from crowded locations, every year I spend a few days fishing Hazel Bridge when the fishing pressure lightens up, usually in the fall, with midges. For those who doubt that the Hazel Bridge Pool offers challenging trout fishing, I am reminded of seeing friends Gardner Grant and Lee Wulff fishing together at Hazel

Bridge. Both were fly-fishing experts who fished for trout, salmon, tarpon, and more, all over the world; and yet they recognized that the midge fishing at Hazel Bridge was exciting and challenged their angling skills. I was with Gardner one day on the Willowemoc when he caught a large brown trout at the beginning of Sherwood's Flats on a size #22 Griffith's Gnat on 8X tippet, a feat that was greatly rewarding. I measured the trout to be fully 19 inches in length. It is difficult to land a fish that large on 8X tippet, and Gardner was so excited at catching that fish that he later wrote an article about his accomplishment for the *Anglers' Club Bulletin* (of the Anglers' Club of New York).

Previous spread: 17. Hazel Bridge Pool is a favorite of flyfishers, especially those who fish with midges.

1 2

FLIES THAT SINK

It is this unknown, that which we cannot observe underwater, which appeals so strongly to the fisherman who handles the wet fly well. This kind of fishing is much harder than dry fly fishing, for the taking of a floating fly is plainly seen.

SID GORDON, *How to Fish from Top to Bottom* (1955)

Theodore Gordon tied some of the first purely American dry flies, and while a great deal of Gordon's notoriety came from his experiences with the dry fly, he believed strongly that fly fishermen should never abandon the wet fly, and that there was a place for both.

I've followed Theodore Gordon's advice, and of the thirty years of my diaries that I have analyzed, there have been years when I caught more trout on wet flies than on dry flies, ten out of the thirty to be exact. It is also true that the best days that I've had catching numbers of trout occurred when fishing with wet flies.

Trout feed predominantly on the aquatic insects that inhabit the streams and rivers in which they reside. In their search for sustenance, trout are said to feed more frequently below the surface facing upstream, because that is the direction where the vast majority of their food comes from. As trout grow, crayfish and small fish are added to their diet, including minnows, such as sculpins, darters, black-nosed dace, and even small trout.

Experienced flyfishers use wet flies as well as dry flies; and although there are sections of streams and rivers that are best fished with dry flies, there are also areas along those same streams and rivers that are more conducive to the use of wet flies. If I was looking to catch numbers of trout I would fish with wet flies.

Users of the wet fly also have the ability to recognize where and when wet flies would be more productive than dry flies. Riffles or fast-flowing water is ideal; however, wet flies can also be used in pools, as well as in ponds and lakes. When fishing under the surface in slower-moving or still water, it is best to provide movement to the fly with the rod by retrieving the fly as soon as it hits the water.

If there is no activity on the stream's surface it is often best to fish with wet flies: either a pair of wets, or a wet fly and a nymph. Should you spot a rise, there is no need to change to a dry fly, just place your wet flies immediately ahead of the rise and use your rod to give the flies movement.

Streams can be fished more efficiently with wet flies, as they are almost constantly in the water and are being used to prospect for trout across and throughout the stream. A dry fly is often in the air, being false cast to a particular rising fish and given a relatively short drift before needing to be picked up and false cast again.

There are also times when flies can be seen riding on the surface, but no fish are rising; this may mean the fish are feeding below the surface. A tactic that was popular years ago was to fish downstream with wet flies for a distance, then turn around and fish a dry fly back upstream. I've noticed, however, that the wet fly seems to have lost its place in the world of fly-fishing and its use is not as prevalent as it was in the past.

Wet flies are most effective during the months of April, May, and June, which coincides with the time of year when the majority of the major fly hatches are taking place. Water temperatures are rising, which can improve the trout's appetite and digestion. All fish have preferred water temperatures; for trout it is generally concluded to be best between 45 and 66 degrees Fahrenheit. However, trout do feed above and below these temperatures.

Fishing with wet flies is a more tactile method than fishing with dry flies, where you need to focus constantly on the dry fly to watch for a "take." Wet-fly fishing is more relaxing, in that it enables you to search the waters for rises, rather than being fixated on a floating fly. One can enjoy the beauty of nature along a trout stream, or search for rises in a more relaxed manner, fishing while doing so.

WET FLY MOVEMENT

Larry Koller advises, in *Taking Larger Trout:* "The basis, I am certain, of all wet-fly technique is the imitation of active nymphs, small crustaceans, minnows or the simulation of something good to eat in the mind of the trout." Some movement of the wet fly is thus often productive.

Wet-fly patterns are often tied with materials that feign movement; movement is a sign of life, and trout generally eat live objects that inhabit streams and rivers. The use of Hare's Ear dubbing, for example, promotes movement when submerged in water, especially when picked out with a dubbing needle. The softness of hen feathers, or brown or gray partridge hackles that routinely move when placed in the water, or peacock herl used as the body of the fly, can simulate the pulsating gills of a nymph when under water.

Another method of imitating a living creature can be supplied using the rod tip, to impart short darting motions which can imitate an insect or nymph that is trying to escape the jaws of the trout. Most wet-fly patterns include a body, tail, hackle, and wings; although some flies are tied with no wings or tails, such as an Orange Fish Hawk or

18. The hackle of a March Brown Spider pulsates when moving through the water.

March Brown Spider, with just a finely tapered body and soft hackle that can be used to create that pulsating movement when the fly moves through the water.

WET-FLY TACTICS

A. J. McClane, in *Fishing with McClane*, says, "I've proved to my own satisfaction at least that a pair of wet flies will double my chances of a strike."

I don't recall ever fishing with just one wet fly. In the Catskills it is customary to fish with two wet flies; this tactic may be as old as fly-fishing itself and was undoubtedly brought to America from England. One fly is tied at the end of the leader and is known as the stretcher or end fly, the other is tied approximately twenty-four inches above the end fly on a separate section of leader of about seven to eight inches in length, and is known as the dropper. The dropper is kept short in order to keep it from twisting around the leader.

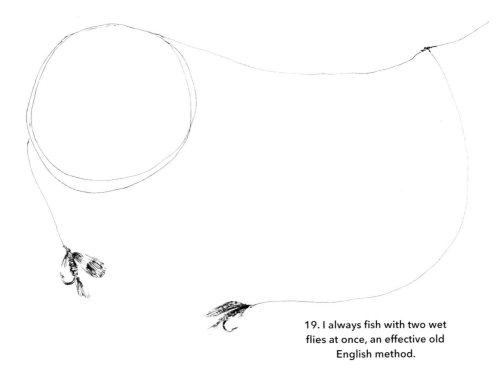

19. I always fish with two wet flies at once, an effective old English method.

One reason for using a two-fly approach is that it gives the trout a choice of two different types of wet flies. Another purpose for using two flies is that two flies produce an action that cannot be duplicated by using only one. The dropper tends to ride closer to the surface and produces a teasing action that is missing when only one fly is used. Usually, a fancy or bright-colored fly serves well as the dropper, such as a Coachman or Royal Coachman. The fly's visibility allows you to stay in touch visually with your flies. A more natural-looking wet fly is used as the end fly, such as a Female Beaverkill, Gold Ribbed Hare's Ear, or Leadwinged Coachman. The strategy is that the bright or fancy fly will get the trout's attention, and if the fish does not take the fancy fly, it might take the more natural-looking fly as it swings past.

It is not uncommon that when a trout takes one of the flies and begins dashing around towing the second fly, a second trout may grab the remaining fly. This is referred to as a "double." Landing two trout on one line is challenging, and the first time this happened to me I was confused as to which fish to net first, as they were pulling in opposite directions. It is best to lead the pair in toward the bank where the water is shallower and then try to get the net under the bottom fish first.

If two different-sized flies are used, the larger fly should be placed on the end, and the smaller on the dropper. This allows for easier and more accurate casting. The same would be true if one fly was weighted, such as a nymph–it should be placed on the end. It's not uncommon to fish a nymph with a wet fly, as it is easier to add weight to a nymph than it is to a wet fly. When fishing with wet flies there should be no false casting. It is best to keep the flies wet so they sink below the surface quickly.

Some advocates of the wet fly believe that it takes more skill to fish a wet fly properly than it does to fish a dry fly; not only are the trout out of sight but so are your flies. When fishing wet, you search for trout with a fly, and learn about trout habitat and how to read water.

As the season progresses and the major hatches subside, stream flows abate and water levels drop, the wet fly can be set aside to be utilized again once a heavy rain occurs and raises stream levels. Many flyfishers mistakenly shun high and discolored water, not realizing that under these conditions trout are very active below the surface of the stream, seeking to feed on the flies and bottom-living creatures that are stirred up with the high flows.

A wet fly with action or movement, darting or dashing across the stream, is more apt to "catch the eye" of a trout than one merely floating on the surface. Heads of pools with fast water and pockets behind boulders are excellent places to fish with wets.

Writing about fishing two wet flies reminded me of a time when I was fishing on the upper Beaverkill near the end of August when stream flows are usually low and clear. However, on this particular day there had been a good freshet the night before and the water was up a little from the rain, and was slightly discolored.

20. The hackle of the Orange Fish Hawk brings life to the fly and is attractive to large trout.

I was fishing with a #12 Orange Fish Hawk as a dropper and a #12 weighted Zug Bug as the end fly. The Zug Bug is really a nymph, but I chose this weighted fly as the end fly to get the dropper deeper. I was fishing at the head of a long, fairly deep roadside pool that was slightly curved and protected by a laid-up rock wall.

On one of my casts a brown trout of about nine inches took the Orange Fish Hawk, and the trout was immediately seized by a large brown trout that had come from under the bottom of the rock wall. The big fish grasped the smaller brown and shook it from side to side, and then retreated back under the wall. I had given the large fish slack and when it settled under the wall, I decided to strike hard and maybe pull the hook out of the small trout and into the jaws of the larger trout.

That didn't work. Instead, the large brown let go of the smaller trout and emerged from under the wall and grabbed the Zug Bug on the end of my leader. After a reasonable struggle I netted both fish; the smaller trout had been mangled and couldn't swim away.

The large trout measured 19 inches and was a beautiful wild brown in excellent condition that was taking advantage of the freshet and feeding near the middle of the day. As I took the fly from its jaw, I also found

21. The 19-inch brown trout that has seized a smaller trout of about 9 inches.

a small madtom in its mouth of about four to five inches; a madtom is a small catfish that lives among the gravel in most trout streams.

I had a good example of how effective fishing with two wet flies can be in an incident that occurred on a small private lake in the Catskills known for its wild brook trout. It was a memorable day as it was also my first day working in the Bureau of Fisheries for the NYS Conservation Department, and it was spent with fisheries biologist Bill Kelly. The lake was located near the headwaters of a Catskill trout stream. The owners had applied for a permit to stock the lake with a species of rainbow trout from the West Coast.

Before issuing the permit the Bureau of Fisheries would conduct a preliminary fisheries survey of the lake and the trout that inhabited its waters. The lake was known for producing abundant numbers of native brook trout that averaged six to eight inches and rarely exceeded nine inches in length. The rainbows were said to be faster-growing and could reach sizes that brook trout could never attain.

Our goal was to sample the existing brook trout population. We needed to get an estimate of abundance, measure and weigh each fish collected, conduct an age-growth analysis, take water chemistry, and determine what impact the new species would have.

We did our water chemistry and proceeded to set a gill net to collect our sample of brook trout. We decided to allow the net to fish a few hours in order to obtain the sample; typically gill nets are allowed to fish overnight and are retrieved the following morning. Bill Kelly believed that leaving the net overnight would result in needless mortality; he brought along a fly rod to help get an adequate sample just in case the gill net was unsuccessful.

The lake was approximately twenty acres in size, and Kelly decided we would row around the lake once and see if we could obtain a satisfactory sample with his fly rod. He attached a pair of wet flies and we each took turns fishing; when a trout was caught, the rod was then handed over to the other person. Once around the lake resulted in a catch of 108 brook trout! We released all the trout, though scale samples were taken from some of the fish for age-growth analysis. When we pulled up the gill net it had a catch of about 20 trout, far fewer than what we caught with a pair of wet flies!

By using wet flies one can manipulate movement, make the fly drift with the current, as well as dart and behave in an inviting manner, which may be beneficial in getting the trout to take the fly. On the other hand, fishing with a dry fly is limited in that after you cast it is best not to move the fly at all, or the fish may spook.

There are several methods of fishing wet flies, the most common being "dead drift." With this method, you cast toward the opposite bank and let the flies move naturally, downstream with the current. At the end of the cast, on the swing, hold the line in your left hand and apply a little movement from the rod with your right hand. If a trout does take one of the two flies the strike will invariably happen when the line is taut on the swing, which takes place near the end of the cast when drag is developed by the current pushing on the line.

When the cast is completed and the line straightens below, it is wise to use the rod tip to move the fly a time or two before picking up the line for the next cast. Trout will often follow the flies on the swing and take the fly when the line straightens out at the end after additional movement has been applied, and the fly moves upward as if it is trying to leave the water. Trout will take the fly on the swing because as it rises from near the bottom it appears to be an insect about to hatch at the surface.

While fishing "dead drift," the left hand holds the line between the fingers and should be ready to keep the line taught should a fish take the fly, as the rod-hand sets the hook. The fingers act as a clutch, and can release the tension if necessary, should a fish strike too hard on the swing. Most of the strikes will come on the swing.

If there is no take by a fish, pick up the line and re-cast. There is no false casting, and the object is to keep the flies wet so they penetrate the water more quickly. Re-cast across the stream and allow the flies to drift downstream again. However, if two or three more casts result in no strikes, take a few steps downstream and repeat casting while covering new water. As a rule, if you catch a trout, or feel a strike but miss, take a couple more casts before moving downstream.

An alternate method to the dead drift is to impart a little movement with the rod tip from time to time as the cast is traveling downstream, even when drag develops on the swing. It helps to alternate between giving the flies movement and not moving them, and there are days when this activity will produce trout. (The difficult part is remembering whether you were moving the fly or not when the fish took.)

Another tactic that can be productive, especially if there is a hatch and the trout are rising, is known as "skittering." Use a small amount of line and work a pair of wet flies just below the surface. After the cast, retrieve the flies with twitching or darting movements that indicate something anxiously trying to get away from the fish. The cast can be made to the opposite side or, better yet, to a rising trout. While moving downstream, the left hand holds tension on the line as the right hand manipulates the rod backward in short pulsing strokes. Generally, the amount of line used is what can be picked up in a back cast.

A similar method of dropping the flies close to a rising trout and imparting movement works well when fishing still waters, such as in beaver ponds, or lakes. In these situations, the trout may act instinctively, to seize the fly before it gets away.

Although fish may be taken in ponds or lakes by casting blindly, fishing is more productive when casting to a rising trout. Try to cast quickly where the rise was before the trout moves, and apply movement to the flies immediately, with short twitches of the rod tip. If you can cast your flies to the rise accurately and quickly, the trout should impulsively take the offering.

In fast water the current gives the flies movement; conversely, in slower water the angler needs to give life to the fly by moving it, yet limiting the amount of time the trout sees the fly. Wet flies can be fished downstream, across stream, or upstream; the object of fishing upstream would be to get the flies deeper without using split shot. This can be accomplished by casting upstream and slightly to the right, say to the one o'clock position, to prevent the flies from floating down directly toward where you are standing. As the flies approach you, try to take in line with your line hand at the same rate of speed as they are moving; then as they float by, point the rod tip slightly down toward the water and slowly shake out line as they pass to provide a longer drift and cover more water. If you are unsuccessful in getting a trout to take either fly by the time the line is straightened below your position, pick them up and repeat the process.

Another tactic to improve your chances of catching trout with wet flies is mending the line. Mending line can add depth, as carefully picking up the moving line with the rod and placing the slack back behind the line enables the flies to move deeper, giving added depth to the cast. This motion is natural for emerging nymphs that come from the stream bottom to the surface, and many strikes occur just at the moment the swing is finished. At times the trout will hook themselves because there is no slack.

THE ROYAL COACHMAN

As stated previously, it is best to use a brightly colored wet fly like the Royal Coachman for the dropper, as the white wing is clearly visible in the water, enabling you to locate your flies more easily. The Royal Coachman is often taken on the first cast. The sudden appearance of this colorful fly may pique the trout's interest and appeal to the trout's impulses.

I use the Royal Coachman more than any other wet fly. The fly has always been a conundrum to flyfishers who believe in imitating the natural fly. There is no natural insect that even comes close to looking like a Royal Coachman, yet the pattern is tied as a wet or a dry, a bucktail, streamer, and even a nymph. The fly is actually sort

22. I use the Royal Coachman more than any other fly; its bright colors are especially attractive to the trout.

23. The Leadwing Coachman wet fly was second only to the Royal Coachman in taking trout.

of gaudy, featuring red, white, and green colors. It imitates nothing in nature, yet the Royal Coachman has a reputation of being a remarkable pattern for trout, no matter how it is tied.

My angler diaries reveal that the Royal Coachman captured more trout than any other wet fly. The fly is a descendant of the Coachman, an English wet fly pattern, though the Royal Coachman is an early American fly, first tied in 1878 by John Haily, a professional fly-tyer from New York. Eventually the pattern was also tied as a dry fly, allegedly by Theodore Gordon, one of the first to tie American dry flies.

My success with wet flies is evident in the diaries covering the span from 1972 to 2001. During this period I took 3,823 trout on wet flies, and as with dry flies, most of the trout caught were taken on a trio of patterns, with the most dominant being the Royal Coachman at 2,842 or 74%, followed by the Leadwinged Coachman with 599 or 15.7%, and the Cowdung, an old English pattern, with 107 or 2.8% trout caught. Although I used a total of thirty different fly patterns, these three patterns accounted for a total of 3,548 (93%) of all the trout caught on wet flies in the thirty-year period.

STREAMERS AND BUCKTAILS

Streamers and bucktails are imitations of small fish, mostly minnows, which are preyed upon by larger fish. Trout are attracted to the movement of the feathers and the darting motion which deceives them into believing the fly is a small minnow.

My experience in fishing with streamers and bucktails began at about the same time that I started fly-fishing. Though I didn't use them very often on streams and rivers for trout, there were times when they brought me moderate success.

The secret of success with streamers is to keep visual contact with the fly, as there is no tension on your line to alert you that a fish has taken the fly. All that is necessary is to set the hook with the rod.

When I first started using these flies, I had caught a few fish when stripping in the fly with a hand retrieve; if there was a swirl where I thought my fly was, I would set the hook with the rod. Then one day

24. Most of the trout I caught on streamers were taken on the Vamp.

I stood on top of a large rock in order to better see my fly, and after making a cast I was able to maintain visual contact with the streamer and could see fish striking the fly. I couldn't believe how many fish hit the streamer on each cast while moving the rod to imitate a minnow darting or swimming. When I kept visual contact with the fly it was easy to set the hook when the fish took the streamer, and my success immediately improved.

My diaries recorded the following information on streamers and bucktails during a thirty-year period:

STREAMERS AND BUCKTAILS

1. Blacknosed Dace (Flick) #12 = 1
2. Black Ghost #4 = 1
3. Black Ghost # 6 = 14
4. Black Ghost #8 = 2
5. Mickey Finn #6 = 1
6. Muddler Minnow #6 = 1
7. Vamp #4 = 2
8. Vamp #6 =81
9. Vamp #8 = 115
10. Vamp #10 = 34
11. Total = 252

As can be seen, most fish were caught on a streamer known as the Vamp, which can be found in J. Edson Leonard's book *Flies*. The pattern is as follows:

VAMP

WING: cream saddle or neck hackles
HACKLE: badger-collar type
BODY: white wool, silver tag
TAIL: black forked tail

While I strictly adhere to the pattern, I do not make the black tail forked, preferring to tie the hackles of the tail in the more common style. I use black silk thread on size #6 and #8 Mustad streamer hooks.

Although streamers can be fished in any month of the year, September is the prime time to use them, as there are an abundance of minnows, as well as young-of-the-year fish and fingerlings, in the rivers and streams of the Catskills. Some of the more common species of minnows that are found in these waters include black-nosed dace, sculpins, cutlip minnows, Johnny Darters, and golden shiners.

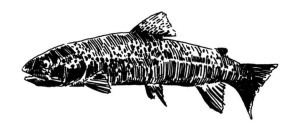

1 3

FISHING WITH NYMPHS

In the early part of the season, before the natural fly is on the
wing, the leader should be weighted, either by lead wire or
split shot, so that the nymph can be worked close over the bottom.
This is the place where brown trout lie, especially if the temperature
of the water is from 40 to 45 degrees. Nothing will induce them
to rise, therefore we must go down after them.

CHARLES M. WETZEL, *Practical Fly Fishing* (1945)

Many wet and dry flies are patterned to imitate mayfly nymphs and adults which hatch each year in late spring and early summer in immeasurable numbers.

In their journey to the surface mayfly nymphs leave the stream bottom and make their way upward through flowing water, eager to reach the surface. During this time nymphs are helpless, and are subject to being intercepted by trout and other fish as they move through the water column. At the surface, the nymphs are again vulnerable as they ride the surface film, split their nymph case, and become what trout fishermen call duns (subimago). When their wings dry they leave the water and seek shelter in nearby trees and streambank vegetation. Within hours the duns shed their skin and transform into spinners (imagoes). The males form a swarm just above the water, into which the females fly to mate while in flight. After mating the females fall onto the water's surface and lay their eggs.

These flies are a favorite of anglers who eagerly await the time of year when they hatch in late spring and early summer. The nymphs all have four to seven pairs of gills on the back of their abdomen, with two or three tails. Some mayfly nymphs live from several weeks to a year or more on the stream bottom where they must avoid being consumed by other insects, trout, and other fish before they emerge, metamorphosing from the nymph stage to the adult stage as a winged insect.

Some species of mayflies will produce several generations in one summer, such as *Isonychia,* which are a major part of the food supply on Catskill trout streams. *Isonychia* nymphs are expert swimmers, agile, and streamlined; they dart about the stream like miniature minnows. *Baetis* nymphs are also fish-like, darting swiftly on the bottom from stone to stone; they are one of the most common nymphs found in streams.

When I first began fishing with nymphs I fished them straight upstream in likely places where trout would be: heads of pools, behind boulders, and in pockets that looked inviting. Strike indicators were unheard of, and the practice was to watch the end of your line where it joins the leader; if the line stopped or hesitated you set the hook. There were also times when two nymphs were tied on a leader, as with wet flies, and were fished similarly to how one would fish with wet flies.

Mayfly and stonefly nymphs are generally found in riffle areas where they cling to the stream bottom on and under stones or gravel, logs, and other underwater debris. Their body shape is flattened, which helps refract current, and they have "hold-fasts" on their claws that help them cling to rocks. Some mayfly nymphs are burrowers and, along with midge larvae, inhabit areas where stream velocities are reduced and silt accumulates in pools, settling basins, and small eddies. Additionally these slower-moving stream sections contain caddis larva, pupa, and other aquatic invertebrates that cling and creep along stream bottoms.

There are times when watching and observing how others fish can be a learning experience that can improve your own fishing skills. One day when I was working on the Willowemoc creel census (1969-1970) the river was high and discolored, with the type of conditions that would keep most fly-fishermen from being out fishing, or at least would have stopped fishing when the water became turbid; they might prefer to wait for a nicer sunnier day. At that time, it would have been my choice as well. However, while driving over the Willowemoc Creek through the Livingston Manor Covered Bridge, I spotted a lone fly-fisherman at the head of a pool and stopped to do an interview. As I approached I noticed that he had a fish on that looked to be of good size, and when he slipped the net under the fish I saw that it was a large white sucker.

He was a fly-fisherman, and up until this time I had never caught a sucker on a fly, and was anxious to learn how he was able to do so. We talked and I asked the usual questions: how long had he been fishing today, what was he fishing with, and had he caught or kept any trout. If he had kept a trout, I would have measured and weighed it; and I would have removed a few scales from the trout's side for age/growth analysis.

I stood on the bank and he remained in the water and continued fishing during the interview. He quickly caught a brown trout of about 12 inches in length, released it, and abruptly caught another about the same size. That was followed by a second white sucker and yet another trout that got off and escaped his net. He was fishing with what seemed to be a very short line, with about ten or twelve feet of line extending out from the tip of the rod, attached to a nine-foot leader with a nymph and split shot tied on. At the end of his short drift, he would pick up the line and quickly lob it back upstream. The fact that he was catching suckers indicated his fly was definitely on the bottom.

My work on the creel census taught me that a rising discolored stream was favorable for fishing with bait, especially near the bottom, but I didn't realize it could be equally as good fishing with flies. I realized that this fly-fisherman was utilizing the conditions to work in his favor and was successful in doing so. He was fishing with flies using the same methods as a bait fisherman using worms, and he was catching fish.

As with many fly-fishermen, I had never fished discolored water with flies and split shot, but was now eager to try this new method of fishing with nymphs during high water. Although I was familiar with how to fish the surface and middle regions of a trout stream I was curious to explore the bottom. At the first opportunity, I returned to the Willowemoc "No Kill" section before the river had a chance to drop to a more normal flow. Tying on a nymph and placing split shot about a foot above it, I caught a trout or two but, in the process, lost a couple of flies. I repeated this several times and got hung up again, losing more flies. It was frustrating to keep replacing lost flies and tippet, so I changed tactics and tied on two droppers, the first about

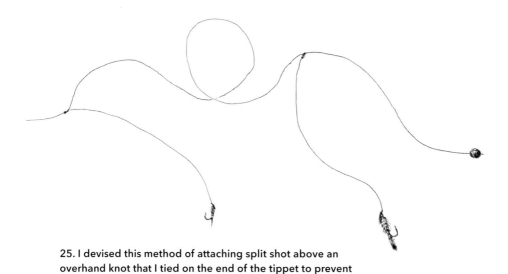

25. I devised this method of attaching split shot above an overhand knot that I tied on the end of the tippet to prevent losing the fly if the tippet got hung up.

eight inches off the bottom and the second dropper about twelve inches above. On the end of the tippet I tied an overhand knot and placed a medium-sized split shot above the overhand knot. (Lead split shot has been banned in New York State since 2004; tungsten can be a substitute for lead.)

I fished with a short line and held the rod straight out over the water, trying to feel either the split shot bumping along the bottom or whether a trout took the fly. This method of fishing nymphs worked quite well, and when I did on occasion get hung up I would lose the split shot, rather than the fly, and was happy with that. My fly of choice became a Zug Bug tied on the bottom dropper above the split shot, and a smaller nymph such as a Blue Quill nymph or Schwiebert's Olive Dun nymph above the Zug Bug.

I learned that this method of fishing nymphs could be utilized any time the flows were higher than normal, regardless of turbidity, primarily during the months of March, April, and May.

Fishing a short line, while holding the rod out horizontally to the water and following the line with the rod, I could at times feel the split shot bumping the bottom; if the line stopped or paused I set the hook.

26. The Blue Quill became a favorite nymph tied on above the Zug Bug with a split-shot rig.

On occasion I would catch a double, and it was satisfying to be able to catch trout when conditions were difficult, despite cold water and air temperatures, resulting in freezing fingers when trying to remove the fly from the trout.

At times I would fish with a nymph and a wet fly instead of two wet flies. I liked to use the Zug Bug as the end fly, not only because it is a good pattern, but because it is weighted, and I want to get the flies down a little deeper. I've regularly used either a Leadwing Coachman or a Royal Coachman as the dropper along with the Zug Bug. This successful combination is usually fished downstream and across the current, with manipulation of the flies by imparting movement or by fishing them "dead drift" on the swing.

The Zug Bug was first created by J. Clifford Zug of West Lawn, Pennsylvania. He first used it successfully in the waters of the Old Red Brick Mill Trout Club that he was a member of in Speonk, Long Island, New York. In 1964 Cliff Zug wrote a letter to the *Pennsylvania Angler* claiming he used a "#10 or #12 hook (2X long if possible), wrapping a few strands of 1.6-inch lead wire over the upper part of the fly. The tail was three peacock sword feathers with a full body of peacock herl and ribbed with oval silver tinsel. The hackle is sparse Coachman brown and two tiny stubs are placed over the hackle"—as the wing case, mallard flank trimmed short, extending over one-quarter of the body.

I fish the Zug Bug often, in sizes #12 and #10 and at times in size #8. I am very particular as to how I tie the pattern. I use Mustad R73-9671 2X long and R73-9672 3X long hooks, and wrap the hook shank with lead wire.

The key to making a good Zug Bug is the peacock herl used for the body. The herl should be taken near the eye of the feather where the flues of the stem of the herl are equally long on both sides of the stem, the longer the better. The herl is wound on edge, one turn in front of the other, making sure not to overlap. The idea is to have the herl flues at right angles to the hook; the longer the herl the more movement there is in the water. I like to use herl large enough that I can shape it with scissors after I tie on the silver oval ribbing. The herl along the abdomen looks like gills on each side of the Zug Bug. Gills control the flow of water through the body and this movement informs the trout that it is a live nymph, not an empty nymph case making its way downstream.

I would not classify myself as a good nymph fisherman. When I think of fishing with a nymph I visualize someone fishing upstream, and casting in the pockets of fast water, with a nymph imitation tied to the end of the tippet. They are casting in likely looking places where trout are located: behind large rocks, in the pockets or small basins where trout can easily hold their positions while looking for drifting nymphs.

When I fish a wet fly it's almost always downstream and I often use a weighted Zug Bug nymph on the end of the leader to help the wet-fly dropper go a little deeper. That is not the same as nymphing; it is wet-fly fishing with a nymph.

Early-season nymphing can be quite productive by concentrating your angling efforts in the deposition areas, where the drifting organisms settle out from the fast water and form a slack-water area off to the side of the main current. These areas will be distinct, since the flow will be much slower there than in the main current. And this is where the trout will be found.

When fishing with nymphs I like to use a 7 ½-foot leader and two droppers. And continuing similarly with what I had learned to do when I first experimented during the Creel Census days, I attach one dropper, approximately eight inches long, about eight to ten inches above the end of the leader, and then attach another eight-inch dropper, ten to twelve inches above the first. I tie the larger nymph on the bottom and a smaller nymph above, then place a split shot at the end of the tippet, leaving the fly above the weight, free to move with the currents.

With this method, if you become "stuck," it is likely the weight rather than the flies that is the problem. When the weight becomes wedged between the gravel and cannot be freed by moving the rod, it simply slides off the end of the leader, which frees up your leader and the flies. It is much easier to replace the weight than it is to tie on a new fly, especially with frozen fingers. One other advantage of placing the split shot on the bottom of the leader below the fly instead of above the fly is that it does not damage the leader. When it's placed above the fly it can pinch or weaken the leader, causing it to break when you have a good fish on.

Don't become discouraged if you are getting hung up on the bottom or catching an occasional sucker along with the trout; when these problems occur, they are indications that you are fishing properly and your nymph is where it should be. I have at times, when I was certain I was hung up, jerked the rod tip frantically in an attempt to free the leader, and unexpectedly had my line start moving slowly away. These instances were caused by large fish that had taken the nymph, and were quite memorable. During the early 1970s I decided to try fishing the "No Kill" water in the middle of winter. I wanted to experiment to learn if trout could be caught at a time when surface water temperatures were in the mid-thirties.

The Willowemoc "No Kill" area is a short walk from where I live, and it is open to fishing all year. The year-round fishing of these waters is permissible because fisheries surveys and population studies revealed there was not much successful spawning; young-of-the-year fingerling trout were rarely if ever collected on stream surveys. It was believed that the adult trout that inhabit the "No Kill" waters most of the year travel upstream during the spawning season.

One late January, on the weekend of January 27 and 28, I tied on a pair of Zug Bug nymphs and added a split shot on the end of the leader to get them on the bottom. While fishing with a very short line, I held the rod tip high, to keep the line short so that I could feel the split shot bumping along the bottom. I followed the line with the rod, and if it paused, or hesitated, I set the hook. I only fished fifteen minutes before I was too cold to continue, but I did catch a holdover brown trout, and that was satisfying.

The next day I fished a little longer and managed to catch two more brown trout, using the same setup. What I believe was important was to keep the line short and to use enough split shot to determine if the flies were on the bottom. I was pleased with my success but waited until March before I fished again.

March is typically a cold month in the Catskills; my diary notes that on March 24, 1973, I had walked along the Willowemoc in the morning. The air temperature was a balmy 50 degrees Fahrenheit, and there were trout rising, taking small dark stoneflies that were having trouble getting out of their cases. In the afternoon I took a water temperature and the thermometer read 44 degrees. I tied a #10 Zug Bug on a dropper above the end of the leader, and a small #16 Schwiebert *Baetis* nymph as a dropper a foot above the Zug Bug, then added a split shot below the dropper. I fished from 1:00 p.m. to 4:00 p.m. and caught eleven holdover brown trout and one wild brook trout. Eight fish took the #16 *Baetis*, and four took the Zug Bug. The following day, March 25, I caught eight holdover brown trout, two on the #16 *Baetis* and six on the Zug Bug #10.

Nymph fishing may not appeal to everyone, but it's satisfying to catch trout on flies under conditions which, while favorable to the trout, demand much of the angler.

14

DRIFT AND DEPOSITION

Mayfly nymphs are an important component of a biological phenomenon known as "drift," the downstream transport of aquatic or terrestrial organisms by stream currents.

GARY BORGER, *Naturals: A Guide to Food Organisms of the Trout* (1980)

Entomologists use the term "drift" to describe the various types of downstream transference of aquatic and terrestrial organisms; they refer to this type of movement as "Constant drift." Trout are the most common predators of drift feeding, which can occur arbitrarily throughout the day at any time of the year; and the term should be of interest to flyfishers. "Surface drift" occurs when adult aquatic insects drift while emerging on the surface, as in a "hatch," or when they return to the surface to deposit eggs.

Perhaps the greatest stimulus for good trout fishing occurs in the early spring with the increase in stream velocity when rivers experience high flows from rains and melting snow. This action causes a large-scale displacement of invertebrates and bottom fauna, known as

"Catastrophic drift." Discolored water is an early sign of "Catastrophic drift" and although many flyfishers pass up fishing during turbid stream conditions, it is one of the best times to fish with nymphs, on the bottom, even when water temperatures are still quite low. In the Catskills, bait fishermen refer to these situations of "Catastrophic drift" by asserting that "the water is just right," meaning it is the best time to fish. It is a time when some of the largest trout in the river are caught after leaving their refuges to devour the available food.

In early spring, when streams and rivers are flowing high and discolored, trout begin to feed heavily below the surface and gorge themselves. The high waters dislodge all types of aquatic insects. Stonefly and mayfly nymphs along with caddis larvae drift helplessly downstream. Many are crushed by the gravel that is also moved by the water; bits and pieces of nymphs accompany those that can no longer cling to the stream bottom because of the increased water velocities. The increased flow causes a rich assortment of trout food to be carried downstream.

A great deal of this food is deposited in distinct areas along the stream, often near the head of a pool, especially on the inside curve of a pool on a bend. Stream velocities are reduced when the water flows into the deeper pool sections; eddies are often formed, and these areas become settling basins, more properly called "deposition areas."

The water at the surface is swifter than that near the bottom. It tends to erode the concave or outer bank on the curve and deposit silt, soil, and drifting aquatic insects into the inside of the curve. These "slack water" areas should be of special interest to trout fishers.

Trout seek this type of habitat, and they are familiar with the stream's hydrology that shifts not only sediment of the stream bed,

27. Deposition areas are often found near the heads of pools on the inside curve of a bend in the stream. They contain a rich assortment of insects and trout food.

but insect life as well, especially in the early part of the season. As would be expected, most of the trout have moved out of the main flow's strong current and are concentrated in the deposition area, not only to rest but also to take advantage of this high-water feast. The trout's stomachs often bulge with undigested nymphs because they do not have to spend much energy obtaining the easily available food. Their digestive processes will be slowed by cold water temperatures. However, even with full stomachs, these trout will continue to feed. Having survived the hazards of a long winter and its sparse food supply, their appetites are large for this unlimited supply of fresh food.

The first step to successful fishing is to find the deposition areas. Fishing can be productive under high water conditions if you know where to fish. In the early spring, and at other times of high water, trout will be gathering in those places seeking the abundance of food, which later in the season will be distributed throughout the riffles and pools. It is best to fish only the slack water, or the deposition area, rather than in the main current. Some of these areas will be more productive than others. The trout are going to be feeding on the bottom, and fishing with weighted nymphs will work best. To be successful you must get your nymph down deep.

Don't give up, even after catching a few fish and the action has slowed. There are more trout to be caught; it can be surprising how many trout will be concentrated in such small areas. I once caught and released sixteen trout on the opening day of the season, in an area approximately twenty feet long and fifteen feet wide. I hardly moved more than ten feet in doing so. I also missed and lost a few fish. This action was on a day when the Willowemoc was so high and discolored that I was the only person fishing the seven miles between Livingston Manor and Roscoe.

This method of fishing nymphs can be very productive, not only in early spring but whenever waters are high and discolored. It is especially effective for catching large trout. Large fish take advantage of feeding opportunities when they occur–which may be why they are large to begin with!

1 5

DO WE EVER
CATCH THE SAME
TROUT AGAIN?

Game fish are too valuable to be caught only once.

LEE WULFF, *Lee Wulff's Handbook of Freshwater Fishing* (1939)

There are times when flyfishers, after releasing a trout, wonder if they will ever catch the same fish again. Those who fish the "No Kill" Special Regulation sections of the Beaverkill and Willowemoc recognize that these areas contain abundant numbers of trout when compared to those places where trout do not have to be released. The fact is that many of the trout inhabiting special fishing sections are caught over and over again, and although hooking mortality does occur, on occasion, these incidents appear to be quite low when compared to the population of trout that live outside the "No Kill" Special Regulation areas. The "No Kill" areas require the use of artificial lures only, such as flies and lures with no live bait allowed, and specify that all fish caught must be released unharmed into the water.

Although some of the trout may carry evidence that they had been caught before in the form of a hook scar, or a missing or damaged mandible on their jaw, a great number of these trout holdover and grow. Generally, if a nine-inch trout is stocked in April and "holds over," surviving the winter and into the following year; it can grow to twelve or thirteen inches in length. And although there are also wild brown, rainbow, and brook trout in the "No Kill" areas, these fish tend to head upstream to the cooler headwaters to spawn, leaving the bulk of the adult trout population comprised primarily of hatchery brown trout holdovers.

It is difficult to recognize if you have caught a particular fish before unless there is some type of physical mark, such as a hook scar, that is obvious, or a wound that may not have totally healed. I have on occasion left a fly in a trout while attempting to net the fish, and the next day, or even a short time later caught the same trout with my fly in its mouth.

There were times when I recorded these types of angling incidents. On May 4, 1974, I made note of such an occurrence that happened on the lower Willowemoc "No Kill" area. It was a day when I had to stop fishing by 3:00 p.m. because of a dinner engagement, and so I kept looking at my watch. Hendricksons began hatching in great numbers about 1:30 in the afternoon and the trout were working like bluefish off the Jersey shore. According to my diary notes, "Caught 20 brown trout, 15 holdovers, 3 hatchery and 2 wild, all on #16 and #14 Adams, most of the holdovers averaged 12" to 14". The water was covered with Hendricksons." While fishing with the #14 Adams and having great success, I caught one brown trout with a hook and worm in its mouth attached to about two feet of monofilament–despite the fact that the use of bait is prohibited in the "No Kill" section. What I found interesting was that even with this burden the trout still took my dry fly; after netting the trout I freed the fish from its inconvenience.

Trout continued to rise and feed aggressively, and I would catch a fish and look at my watch to keep track of the time. At one point I caught a holdover brown trout of about 13" on a size #14 Adams that had a nicely tied size #14 Quill Gordon dry fly stuck in the fish's left maxillary, a bony structure located on both sides of the upper jaw. Flies caught in the maxillary can be difficult to remove because it is bony. The fly was unusual in that it was tied on an upturned eyed hook, a hook that is not seen very often. I tried removing it, but had no luck. I noticed that there was no sign of any leader attached to the Quill Gordon and I assumed that whoever had caught the fish had also tried to remove the hook but couldn't, and snipped off the tippet at the eye of the hook.

Once again I took a peek at my watch and noted the time. There were still a lot of trout rising and enough time to catch a couple more. After a fish or two, I was netting another brown trout holdover and noticed the Quill Gordon with an upturned eyed hook imbedded on the left side of its mouth! I looked at my watch– only twenty minutes had passed since I had first caught the same trout on the same #14 Adams. I assumed it was the same fish I had caught previously as it was highly unlikely that there could have been two trout feeding in the same location, each with a #14 Quill Gordon with an upturned eyed hook caught in its left mandible! As a fly-fisherman I've often wondered how long it would take to catch a trout that was released, and whether a released trout would take the same fly again. In this instance it was just twenty minutes!

Trout, like all predators, are opportunistic and when food is available they need to take advantage of the situation. Sometimes when doing so they get careless, especially when there is an abundance of food. I believe that if you don't over-stress the fish while playing or reeling it in and removing the hook, the experience is quickly forgotten.

A couple of months later on July 8, I recorded another such incident that occurred while fishing the upper Willowemoc Creek, just upstream of Livingston Manor. I had caught a couple of wild brook trout as well as three wild browns and three hatchery brown trout, all on a size #16 Adams. I then noticed a trout rising on the opposite side of the stream from where I was standing. The fish was rising steadily, but was located under a branch that was just a few inches above the water's surface. In order to get the fly in front of the trout I needed to cast further upstream than I would ordinarily, to allow the fly to drift down under the branch to where the trout was rising. On my second cast the fish took; it was a holdover brown of about twelve inches. When I examined the fish I noticed it had a missing adipose fin. (The adipose is the small fatty fin which is located immediately behind the dorsal.) Some trout that are stocked are "fin clipped"--a fin is removed at the NYS hatchery for later identification during DEC stream surveys. (In fact, I may have been the employee who fin clipped the fish at the hatchery!)

In this instance the fish was stocked a year earlier in the "No Kill" area, which was about two miles downstream of where I was fishing. The brown was marked and stocked as a yearling of about nine inches in length, and it had grown approximately three inches since it was placed in the Willowemoc. Obviously, some of the trout placed in the "No Kill" area do not stay where they are stocked!

28. It's difficult to determine whether you've caught the same fish again unless there is an identifying characteristic, such as a scar or missing fin.

I released the fish and watched it swim back across the stream, near the low hanging branch. I happened to look at my watch and noted the time. I kept the same fly on, and noticed a trout rising again under the branch. I cast above it and let the fly drift downstream under the branch as it had done before, and struck as a fish took the fly. As soon as I netted the fish I knew it was the same trout that I had released, the fish with the missing adipose fin. I had caught the same fish twice in eight minutes, on the same fly. I believe instances like this happen more often than we realize, but we rarely have the means of identifying the trout.

On May 30, 1998 I recorded an incident that occurred on the upper Beaverkill while fishing with two friends. One had hooked a fish on an Adams that broke off. He then caught a brown trout on a #14 Royal Coachman Bivisible which had in its mouth the Adams that the fish had broken off fifteen minutes earlier! I had given him both flies.

While fishing the Willowemoc "No Kill" area two years later on July 4, 2000, my diary entry revealed that I "broke off a size #18 Adams & 5 minutes later caught the trout on a size #16 Adams." It's not just the smaller trout that can be caught again so soon after being released. On another occasion while fishing the East Branch of the Delaware one evening at the head of a pool, I caught a large brown trout close to the far bank. When it was netted and measured the trout was twenty inches and was identifiable by an awful-looking hook scar on the left mandible. The scar was old and well healed but was unsightly. A trout of this size is special; it is either faster-growing, longer-lived, or warier than other fish. Generally the larger the fish, the less apt it is to be returned to the water, thus the scarcity of twenty-inch trout.

I caught this fish on June 7, 1998, and noted in my diary: "Fished East Branch, caught 3 hatchery brown trout, 2 holdover brown trout (1-16"), 1 wild brown trout 20" and 1 wild rainbow trout on #14 Adams. Tremendous numbers of #18 and #20 very dark mayflies, Baetis in afternoon 12:30 – 3:00. Tremendous numbers of Sulphurs #14 in evening 7-9 pm."

The next day I decided to go back to the same water where I had good fishing and assumed it should still be productive: My diary entry of June 8, 1998 stated: "Fished East Branch, caught 2 shad #14 Adams, 3 wild rainbow, 17", 19", 19 ½" #14 Adams, and 1 wild brown trout 20" #14 Adams. The brown is the same fish I caught last night, (in the same location, close to the bank on the opposite side) had a nasty hook scar on left side of jaw. Unmistakably the same fish. Not as many flies but enough to have fish rising. Great night! The 19" rainbow trout jumped 11 times!"

Once I caught a trout with a hook point and bend coming out its vent with a snelled leader sticking out of its mouth. The hook got caught on my net and pulled the leader into the trout's digestive system, so I carefully pulled the hook gently and the leader came through the fish, along with the hook. Many times I have caught trout with a hook or monofilament coming out their vent, which shows that these can pass harmlessly through their system.

On a number of occasions I have caught trout with someone else's fly in its mouth and, from time to time, my own fly. I believe that we do catch many of the same trout again, however it may be difficult to distinguish one fish from another of the same species without unusual identifying characteristics.

16

TAKE A
TEMPERATURE
FOR TROUT

Temperature is a necessary factor not only with respect to trout, but
also with respect to many of the forms of life necessary to trout.

HENRY INGRAHAM, *American Trout Streams* (1926)

Trout can be caught throughout the trouting season. Understanding
water temperature and its effect on trout can at times make the
difference between having a successful fishing experience or not. There
are times of the year when it can determine whether or not you should
even be fishing, as well as which type of flies you should be fishing with.

The temperature of water directly influences a trout's appetite
and activity, as well as its metabolism, growth, and reproduction. If
the temperature is too low, trout become inactive; but as the water
temperature rises and becomes too high, the dissolved oxygen in the
water is reduced, and can also contribute to inactivity. It's always a
good idea to carry a stream (water) thermometer in your fishing vest,
especially during the summer months, as well as when you are fishing

streams or rivers that receive cold-water releases from water-supply reservoirs.

In the Catskills there are seven major trout streams that are affected by cold-water releases from New York City reservoirs. Each impoundment maintains a minimum downstream flow by releasing water from the bottom of the reservoirs with temperatures at approximately 39 to 41 degrees Fahrenheit. These cold-water releases directly affect many miles of trout fishing downstream of the reservoirs on the Neversink, East Branch Delaware, West Branch Delaware, Delaware River, Esopus, Schoharie, and Rondout Creeks.

At times these temperatures can change dramatically in a matter of hours; the temperature at Deposit on the West Branch just below the reservoir at Cannonsville can be 50 degrees, but approximately 14 miles downstream at Hancock, can register 60 degrees. The water becomes warmer the farther downstream you travel; anglers may find the main stem Delaware River at Lordville registering as much as 75 degrees. The water temperature in these three locations can vary greatly, depending on air temperatures, sunshine and how much water is being released from the two New York City reservoirs. As a rule, the closer you are to the reservoir's bottom releases, the colder the water.

All fish species have preferred water temperatures; for trout it is generally concluded to be best between 45 and 66 degrees. However, trout do feed both above and below these temperatures. For smallmouth bass preferred temperatures range from 65 to 70 degrees, and for largemouth bass, 65 to 75 degrees. To illustrate how fish species tend to reside together within their preferred water temperatures, I realized that in all the years I fished with two wet flies and caught two trout at the same time, and also caught two smallmouth bass simultaneously, only once in my life did I ever catch a double of one trout and one smallmouth.

Water temperatures are never too cold to catch trout on flies. Good trout fishing can be had in early April when stream temperatures are often 33 and 45 degrees. Fishing with nymphs on the bottom with split shot can be quite effective, especially when flows are high and the river is discolored by rain or melting snow. Fishing with a short line, split shot and short upstream casts gets you to the bottom and aids in fishing nymphs slowly. Although trout will gorge themselves at these temperatures, they seem unwilling to move or chase flies. Perhaps that is the reason wet flies do not produce as well as nymphs when temperatures are below 45 degrees.

On bright sunny days before snow runoff, trout can often be found rising to midges in the slower pool areas. At times good numbers of fish can be seen rising, despite the ground being covered with snow and cake-ice piled along the stream bank, with water temperatures at 33 to 34 degrees. At these times a size #22 dry fly (midge) fished on 6X or 7X tippet will produce good, early-season dry-fly fishing. I have seen trout midging on the Beaverkill and Willowemoc rivers every month of the year except February.

The months of May and June are the prime months for fly-fishing; this is a time that brings together rising water temperatures, abundant fly hatches, and adequate rainfall. (Catskill streams and rivers depend on rainfall, and taking water temperatures at this time of the year is often unnecessary.) This combination provides the ingredients that enable flyfishers to catch more trout more easily than at other times of the season. As water temperatures rise, trout require more food; their body processes are accelerated, and digestive enzymes work more rapidly. Trout appetites are increased and, accordingly, more energy is used. The abundant fly hatches of early summer occur during this opportune time, and with the rising temperatures, trout feeding activity is at its peak.

Conversely, when water temperatures drop, these processes are slowed and trout require less food. Water temperatures change very little on overcast or rainy days, while on clear sunny days they will often rise ten degrees or more, even in the months of May and June. The highest increase I have ever recorded on a free-flowing stream was 17 degrees between the hours of 7:00 a.m. and 4:00 p.m. Water temperatures usually drop one or two degrees at 7:00 p.m. and proceed to drop, with the lowest recording normally being near sunrise.

Trout are cold-blooded animals; their body temperature adjusts to match the temperature of the water they are living in. Water temperatures directly affect their growth, reproduction, and survival. Trout survival often depends on the rate of temperature change, how well the trout are acclimatized as well as the genetic strain and size of the fish. Fortunately, temperature changes on most of our streams and rivers do not occur rapidly. Trout can survive temperatures in the mid-80s but it is generally accepted that they cannot survive them for long. They can live at temperatures above 68 degrees only if the water is well-saturated with oxygen. Temperature tolerance decreases as the oxygen in the water drops.

Brook trout are less tolerant of high water temperatures than are browns or rainbows. Lethal limits are generally accepted to be 77 degrees while the lethal limit for browns is usually placed at 83 to 85 degrees. For rainbows it is slightly higher.

Use a thermometer regularly and learn to understand its messages. Become familiar with taking stream temperatures and do so at a reasonable distance from the stream bank. It is not necessary to wade to the middle of the stream or place the thermometer on the bottom. Make sure you are in flowing water. Shield the thermometer from direct sunlight by shading it with your body, and leave it in the water when taking the reading.

Remember, the warmest temperature will usually be at 4:00 p.m. then gradually become cooler. On the rivers I fish, I have learned what methods of fly-fishing will work best at various water temperatures. My favorite is 66 degrees; at that temperature, even without a hatch, trout are looking to feed and I can usually move fish. They may come up to a dry, take a nymph, or be coaxed into activity chasing a wet fly or streamer. When there is a hatch, the 66-degree temperature can produce the type of day that is memorable.

I find that trout are not as active between 68 degrees and 69 degrees unless there is some fly activity. At 70 degrees a hatch or some flies on the water is practically a must. It is more difficult to tempt trout into coming up for and taking a dry fly by "fishing the water" at these temperatures, or to take them on nymphs or wet flies. I have caught brown trout as well as rainbows under these conditions but that is the limit for trout feeding activity.

Many of our trout streams are subject to extremes in temperature, from a low of 33 degrees in winter and early spring to a high at times in the mid-80s; even such famous Catskill rivers as the Beaverkill, Esopus, and Willowemoc are not immune in some years to 80-degree water temperatures during the heat of summer for short periods of time.

When streams rise above 70 degrees, trout will sometimes concentrate in spring holes in the stream and off tributary mouths. They do so because they are in distress, either from insufficient oxygen or high water temperatures. Trout are very vulnerable at these times, and serious exertion under such conditions may be fatal. I know of no quicker or easier way to impact the trout population in a stream or river than to fish for them when these conditions occur. Similar to fishing for trout when they are spawning, it offers no real sport; rather, the angler is just taking advantage of the fish. Most of these highly vulnerable, concentrated trout that are caught under these conditions do not survive, even if they are released.

When water temperatures are too warm, there are choices that can be made in order to fish for trout: the first and most obvious thing to do is to travel upstream where the water may be more shaded and better influenced by cold springs and cooler tributaries. Another tactic would be to fish a smaller, cooler stream or headwaters; many offer excellent fishing, especially for wild trout.

If your interest is primarily in fishing larger rivers, check out the rivers with cold-water releases. These offer excellent trout fishing when natural flowing streams and rivers get too warm. Tailwaters, as they are sometimes called, occur on many rivers that have been impounded for hydroelectric power or water supply. As previously stated, water is released from the bottom of the reservoirs and is generally colder than the water entering the reservoir. Taking water temperatures on tailwater streams is important, as most of these waters do not have constant steady releases. Flows fluctuate dramatically causing significant changes in water temperatures.

When summer water temperatures rise on free-flowing streams like the Beaverkill or Willowemoc, due to a lack of rain and low water conditions, tailwater streams can offer a "second season" during the summer months.

It is good to remember that these same 39 to 41-degree temperatures that provide such favorable cold-water flows in summer, will actually provide warmer flows in the early spring, when many of the free-flowing streams are running high and cold due to melting snows and ice. I've seen water temperatures in the East Branch in early April that were 10 degrees higher than those on the Beaverkill and Willowemoc. That 10-degree difference on the right type of day can be very important in the early part of the season.

Over the course of time, cold-water releases have caused changes to fish habitat and also to fish populations located downstream of the reservoirs. This has occurred most notably on the White River in Arkansas and on the Delaware River in New York and Pennsylvania. Both rivers had a smallmouth bass fishery prior to dam construction; on the White River water releases improved the flows and lowered water temperatures to 52 degrees year-round, and the colder water changed the fish population from a predominantly smallmouth bass fishery to a world-class trout fishery.

The Delaware also contained a healthy population of smallmouth bass prior to the construction of dams for New York City water-supply reservoirs on both the East and West Branches of the Delaware. While trout, particularly rainbow trout, were present in the Delaware before dam construction, the colder stream flows displaced the smallmouth bass population, sending it further downstream. It greatly improved the trout fishing and today is responsible for making the upper Delaware renowned for its rainbow-trout fishery.

17

CATCHING
LARGER TROUT

*It's entirely probable that the trout fisherman's first big
fish will be encountered in a small stream.*

LAWRENCE K. KOLLER, *Taking Larger Trout* (1950)

In the world of fly-fishing, it is common to hear stories about how "the biggest fish always seem to get away," and in fact they often do. I believe that this occurs because the majority of fly-fishermen are not prepared for catching large trout. However, the opportunity exists on any occasion you fish. Surprisingly, even small streams can hold a big fish, as long as there is good habitat, with sufficient depth and size to provide the fish with shelter and safety from predators. In addition, tailwater fisheries below the reservoirs can harbor large trout; at times reservoir fish will spill over the dam and take up residence in the river below.   I have found that there are definitely more large trout inhabiting our rivers today than years ago. Here are a few suggestions and tips that I have learned from my experiences catching larger fish.

When setting the hook, one needs to be quick but not too physical. There is a lot of stretch in the process: stretch in the leader, in the line, and in the bend of the rod. Strike too hard and you might pull the fly out of the trout's mouth or break the tippet. Your choice of rod can help: bamboo or fiberglass rod tips are generally soft and can "bow to the fish." They are more "forgiving" than other rods, such as those made of graphite, some of which react much too quickly, and can result in missing the fish by pulling the fly out of its mouth. In addition, being stiffer, graphite rods are less forgiving, and can cause the trout to break off or pull free.

Many flyfishers develop bad habits when it comes to handling a trout on the end of their line. We often see them playing a fish by holding the rod in one hand and stripping in, or letting out the line with the other. This often results in a tangled line, especially if the fish decides to make a dash to free itself. The line may become tangled around your legs or rod or net or even tangled on rocks or sticks that are nearby. It will result in losing the fish as the tangle becomes a point of resistance.

The reel does this job more efficiently, feeding the line out evenly, and keeping it out of the angler's way. Your odds of landing the trout increase once you get the fish on the reel; if the trout decides to flee, the line will be released smoothly. Allow the fish to run, this will tire it more quickly, and will enable you to land and slip your net beneath it more easily.

When the fish slows, you can apply gentle pressure by reeling in. If the fish swims toward you rapidly, raise your rod high to maintain contact with the fish while reeling in, and walk backward to take up the slack.

Be aware that more than one run may occur before you have a chance to net the fish. If you become accustomed to playing all fish from the reel you will be ready when you hook a large trout, and your chances of landing the fish will be much greater.

29. If the fish swims toward you rapidly, raise your rod high to maintain contact while reeling in.

Larger trout have exceedingly more strength than average-sized trout, and it is a mistake to attempt to net a large trout while standing in fast water. Even if the trout becomes limp, the weight of the fish alone can be too much for the leader's tippet, or the hook can pull free from the fish, depending on how well it is hooked. Once you recognize that there is a big fish attached to your line, it is better to wade toward shore behind you where the water is shallower and calmer; here the trout will be easier to net when it tires.

I've found that using a net will also increase your chances of landing the fish. Many times a fish will be reeled up, only to dash away from you as you attempt to remove the fly and will often break free and result in a lost fish. In addition, a net can be helpful when handling a fish as many anglers unwittingly squeeze the fish when removing the fly. If you use a net, hold the trout from outside the net as it offers a better grip and aids in getting the fly out of the trout's mouth. It is best not to squeeze the fish especially in the area just behind the head; this is where the trout's vital organs are located.

It is conceivable that a large trout may not fit in the net. If this is the case, a better option may be to beach the trout. If you decide on beaching, choose a shallow area, ideally with a sandy section of the shoreline where the trout can be led onto the shore; the fish's swimming motions may cause it to beach itself. Be sure there are no fallen branches, large rocks, or vegetation in which the fish can become tangled. I prefer this method to using a net if the trout is a large one that I don't want to lose.

A twenty-inch trout caught in a stream or river is the hallmark of a big fish. Most likely the fish is special; it may be faster-growing or longer-lived, or perhaps is just warier and more difficult to catch. It seems as though there are more hallmark trout being caught in recent years. One explanation for this is that today's anglers have experienced fishing in the "No Kill" Catch-and-Release special regulation areas, and are accustomed to returning the fish they catch, releasing both large and small trout in the stream. In years past, before there were

Catch-and-Release areas, larger trout were less likely to be returned to the water; and often, if a large fish was caught it was kept, simply as proof or evidence that a prize fish was taken! However, in recent times an interesting phenomenon has occurred that has become important to the return and survival of these large fish: most anglers today carry cell phones with cameras, and more large trout are being returned to the water unharmed than in the past. Sending out a simple photo on a cell phone will suffice, leaving many more good-sized trout to grow and fulfill their life expectancy. This is also important for the future of wild trout: larger fish carry more eggs and heightened genetics when they reproduce in the fall, and these "hallmark" trout that have survived and grown to a great size are the type of fish that are desired to populate our rivers and streams.

30. More 20-inch "hallmark" trout are being returned to the water, thanks to the advent of cell phones with cameras.

1 8

THE BIG RIVER

*A river is water in its loveliest form; rivers have life and
sound and movement and infinity of variation, rivers are veins of
the earth through which the life blood returns to the heart.*

RODERICK HAIG-BROWN, *A River Never Sleeps* (1974)

The Delaware River is special. At times it even emanates a distinctive aroma: not offensive, but different from that of other rivers. Perhaps this is due to its aquatic vegetation, its size, or the abundance of bottom cold-water releases it receives from two New York City reservoirs. I've spent more hours fishing the Delaware than any other river, and found it to be the most challenging water as well as the most rewarding.

Because it is so large, wading can be arduous. And as with most rivers, nearly every pool has one side that is better to fish from than the other. There are situations that require one to cross the river–such as wind, depth, cross-currents that do not easily allow for a drag-free float, and glare from the sun. I dislike wind. I can cast in the wind, but my casts are not as accurate or manageable as they should be. I tend to fish with wet flies or nymphs if the wind is too difficult to place a dry fly properly.

The Delaware is wide, and the resulting glare on the water's surface can be a hindrance to visibility: whether to see rising fish, flies on the water, or even your own fly. Sunglasses may help the situation; however, I've had a lifelong aversion to wearing sunglasses and I tend not to use them. Sunglasses are dark, and when I look through them I feel as though I am "missing something," and not seeing the entire landscape as it really is.

There were evenings when I would choose a crossing place, but the approaching darkness prevented me from finding the same location from which to cross back. There were also occasions when I was very close to reaching the opposite side but could not make it because of the depth and the velocity of the current, and I would then have to turn around and try another crossing place in complete darkness. Once when it was totally dark I realized I was wading up the middle of the river instead of working my way across. It was then that I started to place a small pile of rocks on the shore, and if I was successful in crossing in a reasonably straight line, I piled a few rocks on the opposite side as well. Eventually I learned where to cross and where not. Many evenings I did cross in the dark, with a small flashlight, hoping I would make it to the other side. It was always surprising to see, with that light, the numbers of flies floating on the surface. Some were spinners or spent-wings, others were adult mayflies waiting for their wings to dry so they could leave the water.

There were times when a landmark could be used to aid in crossing, such as a really large hemlock tree, boulder, or large rock. One such landmark used as a guide was located on the Pennsylvania side of the river below the junction of the East and West Branches of the Delaware in Hancock. There on the water's edge is a large rock on which someone chiseled "W.R. Sept. 5, 1873." Most likely the inscription was carved by a raftsman, who was floating a raft of logs to Philadelphia. He may have docked his raft for the evening and spent some time marking his location. I use the rock as a crossing point to fish the next pool downstream if there are too many fishermen in the pool above.

31. The Delaware River is large, challenging, and rewarding; I've spent more hours fishing the Delaware than any other river.

Access to the Delaware was, and still is, quite limited for wade fishing. The fishing is challenging, and the best way to fish the river in my opinion is with dry flies. Being a large river, long and accurate casts are often necessary to be successful. There is a lot of water to cover, and while I fished with limited success with wet flies and nymphs in the fast water, it was more productive to search for rising trout and fish with dry flies. When there is no surface feeding or visible rises, I typically fish the fast water with a dry fly, and then the pool or slower water. I tend to become restless standing still and like to keep moving from the fast water to the slow water in the pool, and back and forth.

To the best of my knowledge the Delaware River was never stocked directly with trout by New York State, though certainly many of the tributaries were stocked; and some of those fish would work their way downstream to the main river.

For many years my fishing focused on the Delaware during the prime months of April, May, and June. At these times I made daily trips, mostly in the evening. In July and August the river was dependent on cold-water releases which could be somewhat erratic, and in September I would camp along the river for a couple of weeks. There were years when I recorded an average of 86 trips–trips that ranged from an hour or two long to fishing all day. In early spring there were times when I used a canoe, not to fish from, but to cross with when flows were high.

I found the Delaware River so intriguing that I wanted to learn all I could about it. I would measure all the trout that I caught and at times remove a few scales for age/growth analysis. I've kept accurate records of fishing the Delaware, and learned by reading the scales of individual fish that a 20-inch rainbow trout was typically five years old and nearing the end of its life expectancy.

The number of rainbows I caught that reached 20 inches were one out of one hundred; the largest rainbow that I ever caught measured 23 inches. On that day, my diary reveals that the water was 68 degrees, and I caught five rainbows on a size #14 Adams: measuring 9 inches, 12 1/2 inches, 17 inches, 18 inches, and 23 inches. The large rainbow was very thin and in poor condition, most likely due to the fact that it was near the end of its life. Rainbows of 20 inches were scarce; but fish in the 18-to-19-inch size range were fairly common, supporting the idea that life expectancy was five years.

One of the highlights of fishing on the big river is its size, which enables trout to have plenty of room to "run" (take line off the reel) after being hooked. A rainbow trout of 14 inches or greater has the ability to immediately take all of your line and put you into the backing, sometimes on the first run–especially if water temperatures are favorable. I never realized the importance of having backing on your line until I fished the Delaware. The rainbows travel so swiftly and so far that at times you don't realize that the fish that just jumped out of the water is the one on the end of your line!

The river is a wild-trout fishery that is dependent on cold water releases from New York City reservoirs at Deposit on the West Branch, and at Downsville on the East Branch. With a wild-trout fishery it is common to find that even during a good hatch, the trout do not all feed together at the same time, as do hatchery trout. The Delaware is large and intimidating. It is as wide as three lower Beaverkills, with all of the same hatches: tremendous hatches of mayflies, caddis, large stoneflies and even Dobson flies (hellgrammites), as well as additional mayfly hatches not found on the Beaverkill. When Hendricksons are hatching the water can be completely covered with floating flies, and as a result, the trout have a lot to choose from. Accurate casting is a must, and in every pool there will be trout rising that cannot be reached by wading.

Although food is plentiful and the number of flies riding the surface can be incredible, success is often determined by being able to reach rising fish and staying until late in the day. Those flyfishers who fish the big river regularly put in a significant amount of time learning the complexity of the fishery.

Water temperature often decides where, or if, you should fish. One of the main items that should be included with your fishing equipment is a water thermometer that can be used especially in the warmer months before you embark on a fishing trip. Fortunately, today you can find information on the water temperature and river flows online, but a thermometer is still important to carry along.

Many evenings, after an early dinner, I drove over to the river and was in the water and casting in 25 or 30 minutes. Shortly after sunset, I noticed most fishermen would start reeling in and were ready to call it a day. But as I became more familiar with the river, it was apparent that as the sun was going down, the trout often began rising and feeding on the surface. This caused me to stay later into the evening and, at times, it was as if someone threw a switch and the trout began to rise. I've seen the surface literally covered with floating flies after dark–with hatching duns, and at times spinners or spent-wing flies.

Rainbow trout

19.8″ — 5+ year old

17.8″ — 4+ year old

15.3″ — 3+ year old

11.6″ — 2+ year old

9.7″ — 1+ year old

2.8″ — 0+ year old

Brown
trout

15.6″

5+ year old

13.4″

4+ year old

11.7″

3+ year old

10.2″

2+ year old

8.9″

1+ year old

3.1″

0+ year old

32. I've kept
accurate age-
growth records
of Delaware
trout by reading
scales from the
fish I caught.

Twilight, the soft glowing light emanating from the sky after the sun sets below the horizon, is caused by the scattering and refraction of the rays of the sun from the atmosphere. At this time of the evening, the majority of flyfishers I encountered on the river would have stopped fishing when they could no longer see their fly. They believed that in order to catch fish it was necessary to see the fly, and some even assumed that if they couldn't see the fly, neither could the trout.

I learned early on that trout in the Delaware were indeed able to see my fly, even if I was not, and that trout could be caught as long as you could see the splash or flash of white in the water made from the rise, and could set the hook. The leader size I prefer is 4X, but I add a section of 5X or 6X depending on what hook size I plan to use, and then prepare for the post-evening fishing by cutting the tippet back to 4X before it becomes too dark. During this time of the evening I strike the rise without actually seeing the fly, preferring to use a stronger tippet, as the trout tend to be larger at this time of day and are certainly not leader-shy in the dark.

One evening on the Delaware after dark I hooked what was going to be my last fish before reeling up. It was a small trout, and after playing and netting the fish, I put a pen-type flashlight in my mouth and knelt down to extract the fly. I was surprised to find that the Adams was rather bedraggled and wondered what had happened, as the fly had hardly been used. After removing the hook, I placed the trout in the water and stood up to blow the fly dry. By the time I got my hand on the reel, the line was being pulled back out into the river. I played the fish, netted it, and to my surprise, the flashlight revealed that my Adams was still in the trout's mouth: I had removed someone else's Adams the first time I netted the fish!

Though it is not necessary to see the fly in order to catch trout, it is important to see the rise and to be able to judge the distance between yourself and the fish. With practice, I've had good success at these times because I learned to use my night vision and judge the distance to the rising fish. Trout seem to feed with recklessness after dark; if there was a rise in the vicinity of my fly, I set the hook. This did not always result in catching a fish, but it did far more often than not. Utilizing this method of fishing often turned a fishless evening into a successful one. It became apparent that the trout were not spooky after dark, and even if you struck and missed or made a commotion, the fish continued rising. It generally takes about seventy minutes to become fully dark after sunset, a time of evening I refer to as "dark dark." Your eyes can adjust to darkness and improve your night vision, and having the added opportunity of more time to fish under these circumstances resulted in more success. I heard rises often late into the night when camping along the river.

Trout became easier to deceive as the evening progressed, and poor presentation would be hidden by the darkness. There were times when the only fish I caught occurred at dark. Unfortunately, after catching two or three trout it became too dark to see anything, but to emphasize, seeing the fly is not necessary but seeing the rise is, and I improved at this type of fishing as I gained experience.

Staying until darkness did have one problem–it increased the possibility of meeting up with a Timber rattlesnake, along paths, roads, and wood-roads as well as on the shoulder of the railroad bed. Despite trying to avoid them, on average, I would encounter one to three Timber rattlesnakes each year. If you do see a rattlesnake, do not panic, keep a safe distance, six feet or more, and let the snake move along on its own. Do not kill or collect the rattlesnake. Timber rattlesnakes are not aggressive unless provoked. They are endangered and protected in New York State.

1 9

PRESIDENT
JIMMY CARTER
AND THE CATSKILL
FLY FISHING
CENTER

I agree with the Center's purpose of preserving the heritage
of this special area. There's good fly-fishing in Georgia, but this is
the heart and soul of fly-fishing. This is the Mecca which draws
other fly-fishermen. It's a place I've always wanted to visit.

PRESIDENT JIMMY CARTER,
article by Jan Cheripko, *Catskill/Delaware* (1984)

I've fished the Delaware with many flyfishers; but the most memorable of them all was Jimmy Carter, the 39th President of the United States. President Carter occupied the Oval Office from 1977 to 1981.

Having heard that Jimmy Carter was an avid fly-fisherman, members of the Catskill Fly Fishing Center (the CFFC) sent the former President a letter in the Fall of 1984 asking if he would be their guest of honor

33. President Carter is an expert and knowledgeable trout fisherman.

at the Center's fall fund-raising dinner, and enjoy a few days' fishing. The former President was given the chance to sample the trout fishing along the Upper Delaware and the Beaverkill when he visited the Catskills for a week in September. The Center had purchased a thirty-five-acre property along the Willowemoc Creek, between Livingston Manor and Roscoe, and planned to construct a modern fly-fishing museum, library, and research and demonstration facility.

Mr. Carter replied that he would be happy to be their guest of honor and assist with the building fund. Those in charge at the Catskill Fly Fishing Center were delighted and notified members that both the former President and Mrs. Carter agreed to serve as Honorary Hosts of the fall fund-raising event, as Mrs. Carter was also a very capable flyfisher. I was asked to serve as the Carters' fishing guide during their stay.

When interviewed for the *Catskill-Delaware* publication about his visit, Mr. Carter stated: ". . . the letter I received from them was so enticing that I couldn't resist."

With the Carters was Jack Crockford, a legendary conservationist and director of Georgia's Game and Fish Division, and a longtime friend from Georgia. Though the former president had fished his entire life, it was Jack Crockford who put the first fly rod in his hand. The trio, along with several Secret Service agents, stayed at the Beaverkill Valley Inn in Lew Beach.

The entourage landed at Sullivan County International Airport on September 19, 1984, at about 4:00 p.m. and arrived at the Beaverkill Valley Inn roughly an hour later. A special dinner for the Carters, attended by Catskill fishing celebrities and officers of the Catskill Fly Fishing Center was scheduled for 7:00 p.m. I received a telephone call from Joe Horak, who was a Board member of the CFFC, saying that the President was anxious to fish, even though there was limited time before dinner. I advised Joe to have Mr. Carter fish near Turnwood, and the former President hurried out to the Beaverkill, and caught ten or twelve trout on a size #18 Adams, which confirmed to everyone present that he was a bona fide fly-fisherman.

At the dinner that evening, Mr. Carter came over to where my wife and I were sitting and said he had heard we were married along the banks of the Beaverkill, and that we had two small children (Lee, age two, and Tyler, just four months). He inquired whether he would be able to meet them and said he would like to have his picture taken with them. He did so on his Friday morning visit to the site of the Catskill Fly Fishing Center.

While in the Catskills the former President fished the upper Beaverkill and the Upper Delaware River. He mentioned that he was a life-long fisherman, and that he took up fly-fishing while in the White House. He even tied his own flies, and his two favorite dry-fly patterns were the Adams and a Black Ant tied with deer hair. Mrs. Carter told me that there was a time when Mr. Carter carried *Art Flick's Streamside Guide* with him whenever he fished.

On the second day of his visit Mr. Carter fished the Beaverkill again in the Turnwood area. This was the first day that I guided him, and I realized almost immediately that he knew how to fish. With an entourage of Secret Service agents eyeing his every cast, he successfully plied his skills on a significant number of Beaverkill brown trout. Mr. Carter could read water and place his fly where he wanted it to go; and when the fly was taken, he reacted with a quickness that separated an expert from the average fly-fisherman.

Mrs. Carter also proved that she had fly-fishing talent. She more than held her own, catching a number of trout on the Beaverkill, along with a wily rainbow or two from the Delaware under high-water conditions that veteran flyfishers would have found challenging.

I recognized how eager Mr. Carter was to get out on the river and fish for trout; and yet he gave freely of his time by making several public appearances in Livingston Manor, Roscoe, and Callicoon, in addition to the formal fund-raising dinner. There were lunches and dinners and press interviews and stops here and there; but in between the Carters were able to fish.

34. President Carter is a fearless wader, despite the depth of the river.

Although he spent more time on the upper Beaverkill, there were a couple of trips to the Delaware River. Though he had never fished or seen the Delaware, Mr. Carter had a connection to the river. During his tenure as President, he was responsible for adding 73 miles of the Upper Delaware River to the National Wild & Scenic Rivers System, in November of 1978.

The first day we fished the big river the water level was high due to water releases from the Cannonsville reservoir. The water temperature was favorable at 60 degrees, though there were few flies on the water, and not many rises. The added flow made wading difficult in some places, but Mr. Carter was a fearless wader, and at Dark Eddy we decided to cross the river.

Although there were six or seven Secret Service agents along the riverbank I believed that I was directly responsible for the former President's safety in getting across the river and back again, without going for a swim. Needless to say, I was a bit nervous. I suggested utilizing a tactic of locking arms that had been shown to me and we took off. The river was high due to the added releases, almost to the top of our chest waders, and we came close to "taking on water" both times, but we made it across. Afterward I remarked that now there were two Presidents who crossed the Delaware–George Washington (in a boat) and Jimmy Carter in his waders!

There was not much surface activity. Only a few fish were rising. Mr. Carter was using a #16 Adams and focused on a trout that was coming up to the surface more than any other. He had made several good presentations, and I was surprised that the fish did not take. I suggested that he make a few more casts and then asked him to tie on one of my #16 Adams. He gave a small laugh and said "are you telling me Ed that your Adams is better than the Adams I have on?" I replied no, not really, but on this river, I have a lot of confidence in my flies. He took my Adams and tied it on, and the next time the trout rose it took the Adams I had given him. The fish put him into his backing, and I was delighted to see that it was a hefty rainbow that measured about 16 inches. After removing the fly and blowing off the moisture he asked, "Do you think there is another trout in this fly, Ed?"

We fished the big river twice, but not at the proper times of day. The flows were higher than normal, making conditions difficult, although water temperatures were favorable. Unfortunately, just when the trout began to rise it was time to leave. Mr. Carter was expected at a press conference and dinner at the Antrim Lodge in Roscoe. Although there were five or six cars with Secret Service waiting for him, when we were ready to leave Mr. Carter elected to drive back with me in the front seat of my car. He informed the Secret Service that he was "going back with Ed, we have to talk fishing." The hour drive back was enjoyable. He asked many questions about fishing and my work with the Department of Environmental Conservation. He had a great personality: he genuinely liked people and went out of his way to meet others, especially children.

On the second trip to the Delaware Mr. Carter asked me if I would like to invite a friend to come along and fish. I said yes, and chose Phil Chase, of Port Jervis, New York, and informed him that Phil was an ardent fly-fisherman, conservationist, schoolteacher, and outdoor columnist. Phil had worked diligently for many years, writing about the unregulated water releases in the Delaware water system that caused water temperatures to become too warm, with no consideration for the river's wild trout population, and at times resulted in fish kills of trout as well as other species of fish.

We fished at Dark Eddy after lunch. The river was higher and colder; the water temperature had dropped from 60 degrees to just 52 degrees. There were not many flies, and few fish were rising. Only Mrs. Carter was successful in catching a trout, a rainbow of about 12 inches. She caught the fish on a size #14 Gray Fox Variant I had given her.

That evening a small dinner party with the Carters was held for the Benefactors who had purchased special tickets that included weekend accommodations and fishing on private water.

On Saturday I again met the Carters for breakfast, and we decided to look at Junction Pool on the Delaware. No fish were working and there were quite a few people fishing. When Mr. Carter arrived, we sat on the bank watching the pool. It was a very pleasant time spent together: the weather, the pool, the discussion about fishing, writers, and the like. He stated that he would like to invite me over to fish Spruce Creek with him.

I decided we should fish Boucheaux, and Mr. Carter again rode in my car on the trip downriver. There was no action at Boucheaux, and after fishing a short time, we opted for an early lunch and returned to Dark Eddy, but as on the past trips, had little time to fish. There was no real activity until it was time to leave. At one point I suggested to Mr. Carter to tie on one of my size #14 Royal Wulffs as a prospecting

35. Mrs. Carter was also adept at fly-fishing and was successful in catching trout.

fly. Shortly after doing so, he raised a good fish and played it for quite a while before losing it. The fish were just beginning to rise steadily when we needed to depart for the Gala dinner.

That evening, September 22, 1984, was the Catskill Fly Fishing Center's main event. The fund-raising dinner was held at King's Catering House, located near the Catskill Fly Fishing Center, and was sold out. One hundred forty people attended, and the CFFC grossed between $35,000 and $40,000.

On Sunday morning I again had breakfast with the Carters at the Beaverkill Valley Inn. We returned to the Beaverkill at Turnwood, with Mr. Carter using one of my size #16 Adams and fishing upstream. Mrs. Carter fished downstream. The President caught several trout and then switched to the Royal Wulff and was very successful catching fish.

I decided to say my goodbyes on the stream rather than at the farewell luncheon at the Beaverkill Trout Club. Mr. Carter said he had read about me and my fishing, and did not know what to expect, but was happy "that I was the person that I was." He said the hardest part of the trip was leaving me behind. Mrs. Carter said they talked about me at the end of every day. Mr. Carter stated that he would return and that he wanted to fish the Delaware with Lee. I replied that would not be a problem since Lee liked to fish the big water. But when he realized that I was speaking of Lee Wulff, he replied: "I mean The Lee, your son!"

President Jimmy Carter had a keen personality. He was quick witted, intelligent, and the type of person you looked for in a good friend: he had a great sense of humor. The Carters were kind and caring and were successful in their fund-raising efforts on behalf of the Catskill Fly Fishing Center. Their trip did much to benefit fly-fishermen and the Catskills. Although they never returned to the area, we corresponded throughout the years, always with fond memories of their historic visit.

20

FISHING WITH OTHERS

The angler forgets most of the fish he catches, but he remembers the streams in which they are caught.

CHARLES K. FOX, *The Wonderful World of Trout* (1963)

Years after the Carters' historic visit, on October 20, 2007, retired Supreme Court Justice Sandra Day O'Connor stopped in the Catskills for a day's fishing on her way up to Ithaca for a speaking engagement at Cornell University. I had been contacted a few days before by her group, Stewart Schwab, Cornell Law School Dean, and Mitchell Lasser, Cornell Law Professor, both of whom had clerked for Ms. O'Connor in the past.

The former Justice had been an avid flyfisher for three decades, and regularly took her law clerks on fishing trips each year. While she was in Washington, D.C., the outings were most often on the Potomac River. The Cornell spokesperson explained that Ms. O'Connor wished to visit the Catskill Fly Fishing Center and Museum and had requested a day's fishing. She stated that she was on a plane leaving Montana and happened to meet former President Carter on board. Both had been fishing, and this was a few years after his visit to the Catskills.

During their conversation, Mr. Carter suggested that she "travel to the Catskills to fish with Ed Van Put as guide and visit the Catskill Fly Fishing Center and Museum."

On the day she arrived in late October we had an enjoyable tour of the Center and a picnic lunch. Unfortunately, all the rivers were high, nearing flood stage, but we did manage to wet a line in the Willowemoc by the CFFC and visit the Beaverkill, as well as discuss rivers we liked to fish, President Carter, and fly-fishing in general.

I have been fortunate to have fished with a number of people, including some of the best fishermen and outdoor writers I had admired throughout the years, who have now passed on, such as Harry Darbee, Art Flick, Lee Wulff, Al (A.J.) McClane, and Art Lee. And many of my fondest memories are of introducing people to trout fishing in the Beaverkill for the first time: children, veterans, family members, neighbors, and friends. In addition, there were flyfishers from France, trout fishers from Russia, a Supreme court justice, a former President of the United States, a Japanese Ambassador, a former Chair of the Federal Reserve, the U.S. Secretary of the Treasury, and John Kennedy, Jr.

One of the most exciting experiences I've had on the Beaverkill came about in 1988, when I was a member of a team of American flyfishers who fished with trout fishers from Russia and participated in a fishing contest. This occurred during the end of the Cold War between the United States and the communist Union of Soviet Socialist Republics.

By the late 1980s, the Soviet Union began to change, and a more open policy was introduced by then-Soviet President Mikhail Gorbachev. New freedoms were given to the Russian people; this lessening of restrictions encouraged greater communication between Russians and Americans in business well as in culture.

During the summer of 1986 the American organization Trout Unlimited, and the Rosohotrybolovsoyuz, the All Russian Union of Hunters and Anglers, met in Moscow to work on a cooperative agreement that would allow American anglers to travel to Russia and fish the vast cold-water fishery resources of the Soviet Union. The Russian government believed that by providing fishing opportunities to Americans it would receive an economic boost to tourism; and it was

36. US-USSR Anglers Exchange Group. FRONT ROW, L to R: Dave Pabst, Andre Velikanow, Lev Stroguin, Ed Van Put SECOND ROW, L to R: Ed Sharbonneau (translator) Lee and Joan Wulff, Earl Worsham (TU International), Nelson Bryant (NYT columnist) STANDING, L to R: Sevelo Gnevashov, Leonid Prodanova, Larica Gubanova, Dot and Budge Loeckle, Luda Sharbonneau, (translators), Dick Talleur, Ella (translator), Dale Hardeman (NYC TU president), Aleksandr Klushin, and Gardner Grant (TU International)

hoped that Russians would in turn learn about U.S. fisheries management, tackle, and techniques, as there were very few flyfishers in Russia, and hardly any fly-fishing equipment available to them. The agreement included the exchange of fishing trips between the two nations.

The first angler exchange took place in October 1988, which was hosted by Trout Unlimited. Six Soviet anglers arrived at the Beaverkill Valley Inn in Lew Beach. They were shortly afterward taken to the nearby Joan and Lee Wulff School of Fly Fishing, where they received lessons from Lee and Joan.

One of the conditions of the anglers' exchange was that there would be a fishing contest. The Americans decided that it would be more equitable and fairer to have the Russians and the Americans paired into teams, rather than a competition directly between each country.

The American anglers included *New York Times* Outdoor columnist Nelson Bryant, renowned fly-tier Poul Jorgensen, fly-fishing author Richard Talleur, fly-fishing professionals Joan and Lee Wulff, and myself.

The contest was held on October 25 and took place in the special No-Kill areas of the Beaverkill and Willowemoc. Three teams fished Cairns pool on the Beaverkill, and three fished the Hazel Bridge pool on the Willowemoc. The team that caught and released the greatest number of total inches of trout would be declared the winner.

In order to be designated as an "official competition," judges were procured from the NYS Department of Environmental Conservation: Region 3 Fisheries Manager, Wayne Elliot; and Habitat Protection Biologist, Jack Isaacs, both of whom were experienced flyfishers. They carried long-handled nets, measuring boards, and clipboards to accurately record the catches.

The contest took place on a day that was not well-suited for fly-fishing, with snow and rain causing uncomfortable fishing conditions; nonetheless, at the end of the contest, twenty-two trout were caught, measured, and released.

That evening a special dinner was held at the Beaverkill Valley Inn, which had decorated the dining room tables with small Soviet and American flags. Various state officials and dignitaries, along with a few Soviet interpreters, dined and celebrated the historic event. Speaking with the assistance of an interpreter, Aleksandr Klushin, the Soviet team captain and vice-chairman of the Rosohotrybolovsoyuz, announced that he and his teammate, Ed Van Put, had won the contest. He proclaimed that every year a special award is given to the best fisherman "in all of Russia" and wanted to present that award to me, since I had caught the most trout in the contest. It is an award that still hangs on my wall today.

Throughout the years I fished in the Catskills with friends and acquaintances and, on some occasions, with friends of friends. At times, these were anglers who had never fished with flies; however, as I had spent several years working weekends at the Joan and Lee Wulff School of Fly Fishing as an instructor, I was able to teach them well enough to make these outings productive. Showing a novice angler how to be successful with a fly rod is greatly rewarding.

In the summer of 1991, I had the pleasure of introducing a fly-fisherman from France to the upper Beaverkill, Willowemoc Creek, East Branch of the Delaware, and the main stem Delaware River. My friend, Dan Rather, had told me about Jean-Claude Andres, whom he had fished with in France, and Dan was eager to reciprocate by introducing John Claude to the fishing here in the Catskills. He asked if I would take him fishing and I agreed; we met on the Upper Beaverkill on the last day of May in 1991.

As I drove up the Beaverkill valley to meet him, I thought about what kind of flies Jean-Claude might have brought along with him from France and was curious to see what type of flies he would use. I wondered how the trout were going to react to flies they had never seen before and was curious to learn whether French-tied flies would work on Beaverkill trout. If they did not, I reasoned, I could always offer him some of my flies to use.

Jean-Claude was looking forward to his first fishing experience on the Beaverkill, and I was pleased to accompany him. It was the time of year when trout fishing is at its best, and I could see that he was anxious to get in the river. There were still a few hours left in the day to fish, so we headed out.

At the river Jean-Claude opened one of his fly boxes and asked me to choose a few flies that might work. The fly box was filled with French-tied flies with many using CDC (cul de canard) feathers. None of the flies resembled anything I had ever seen before, and yet they all appeared as though they would float well and would catch fish.

I chose a couple of interesting-looking flies for him to use. There were trout working on the surface, and Jean-Claude immediately started to catch them. His casting abilities revealed that he was a superb flyfisher. He clearly knew how to present the flies he was using, and he fished with confidence. His accuracy with a fly rod was impeccable, and he had no trouble catching one fish after another. By the time we could no longer see our flies, he had caught and released more than a couple dozen brown trout.

The following day I again fished with Jean-Claude, this time on the lower Willowemoc Creek in the Special Regulations area below Livingston Manor. He was very impressed with how good the fly-fishing was in the Special Regulations area. And again, Jean-Claude was successful in catching many more trout on his French flies.

A note in my diary dated June 1, 1991, states: "It is interesting (very) that someone can come here to the Catskills from France and use flies from that country that imitate no hatches in this country, and catch the number of trout Jean-Claude has caught. . . He is 'stream smart' (an excellent caster) and would catch trout anywhere on any type flies."

The following year (1992) Jean-Claude made another visit to the Catskills, although this time he was accompanied by Daniel Maury, the editor of the French angling magazine titled *La peche Mouche*. Jean-Claude, Daniel and I fished the Willowemoc, the East Branch of the Delaware, and the main Delaware River. Unfortunately, the water temperature on the Delaware River was too warm for decent trout fishing, as the cold-water releases from the reservoirs into the river below had not yet begun. However, both were successful in catching trout on French flies while fishing the Willowemoc and the East Branch.

It was also in 1992, in early December, when I first met John Kennedy, Jr. A mutual friend had called and asked if I would meet with John, show him and his friend around the area, and talk about the Beaverkill. We ate lunch along the stream, and greatly enjoyed our time together. He was impressed with the river and the natural beauty of the area and mentioned that he wanted to learn how to fly-fish. I agreed to teach him, and we scheduled the following May (1993) for lessons.

John returned in early May with another friend, and again we spent several enjoyable hours together, beginning with casting lessons in a grassy area near a pond. After John became comfortable with using a fly-rod, we ended up on the river.

My diary entry on May 9, 1993 states: "Beaverkill. Taught John Kennedy Jr. how to fly fish. Spent time 11:30 – 5:00 fishing & casting. Last night Obie (Judy) & I had dinner with John at the Inn."

After the casting lessons were over and we went to the river for his first try at fly-fishing, John hooked his first trout on the Beaverkill.

In addition to the enjoyment that comes from teaching others to fish or introducing them to trout fishing in the Beaverkill, there were learning experiences as well.

In the late 1990s I had the pleasure of fishing with Paul Volcker, former Chairman of the Federal Reserve. Paul had been contacted by Board members of the Catskill Fly Fishing Center and had agreed to donate a weekend of his time to assist in raising funds for their new museum. Paul met with members and served as guest speaker at a special dinner. Part of the agreement included a day's fishing, and I was asked to take Paul to the Delaware River or any other location he desired to fish. We became friends, and we fished together from time to time. On one of our fishing trips he brought along Seiichiro

Otsuka, who was, at the time, the Japanese Ambassador to the United States. The Ambassador spoke flawless English and was an excellent fly-fisherman. He fished with a traditional American fly-rod as well as anyone I've ever fished with. We had a very enjoyable time fishing together, and he asked if I would consider taking him and his wife and son fishing; I replied that I would be pleased to do so.

I met the Otsuka family in mid-June and, despite rainy weather and a rising river, each of them caught several trout. After catching a number of fish that day, "Ichi" as he invited me to call him, went back to the car and returned with three telescoping rods; one made of graphite, another of fiberglass, and the third of bamboo. He attached a wet fly to the line on the end of one of the rods, as there was no reel, and caught fish after fish. He gave me a rod to try, and I immediately caught a rainbow trout. He then presented me with his rod that he called a "Japanese Mountain Stream Rod" as a gift.

My diary entry for Saturday, June 13, 1998, reads: "Fished with Ambassador Seiichiro Otsuka, his wife & son (8 yrs old) Everyone caught several trout. Lots of rain & stream rising. He used a Japanese 20' rod with the line tied on the end . . . and caught brook, brown and rainbow trout on a Royal Coachman wet fly. He insisted I try the rod & on one cast I caught a 14" R.T. (Hatchery). Really neat rod. He also presented his Japanese Mountain Stream rod to me. I can't wait to use it! (12' long)"

I learned that the term often used today for the type of telescoping rod with a fixed line and no reel is "Tenkara." However, the Ambassador was adamant in stating that his rod was not Tenkara but was a "Keiryu" rod, which is the word for Mountain Stream fishing. Keiryu encompasses many types of fishing in Japan, including Tenkara, fly-fishing, as well as fishing with lures and bait.

37. The Japanese mountain stream rod given to me by Ambassador Seiichiro Otsuka along with his favorite wet fly. When fully extended, the rod reaches 12 feet in length.

That summer, I switched from fishing with my fly rod to the Keiryu rod that Ichi had given me and was delighted with the results. At one point I added up my tally after six days of fishing with this rod and found I had caught a total of 132 fish–76 rainbow trout, 43 brook trout, and 12 brown trout. The Keiryu rod felt like an extension of my arm, and I was surprised at how stealthily I could drop a wet fly into a small stream or pool without disturbing the water or the fish below and be rewarded with immediate results.

This type of fishing reminded me of how early trout fishermen like John Burroughs must have fished, by using a willow switch and attaching a line to it. I decided to go and fish the same streams and tributaries that Burroughs had fished in the late 1860s and had equally good success. By using a split shot tied at the end of the line (mono-filament) with a wet fly tied on about six inches above as a dropper, the combination was deadly. There was no line to land on the water as there is when you cast a dry fly. Many times, rather than casting, I

gently lowered the split shot into the water, which was very effective in small streams. It was quite a learning experience.

It was amazing to learn how many more fish than I realized were in the same pools I had fished with my fly rod through the years, and how many more trout I was able catch in those pools with the rod given to me by Ambassador Seiichiro Otsuka.

21

EQUIPMENT OR TACKLE

> *The typical Cummings action has a delicate hooking tip*
> *that rivals all but the finest bamboo, and the thin walled butt*
> *section flexes dramatically into the cork grip itself, like the*
> *best of the Ritz, Garrison and Young parabolics.*
>
> ERNEST SCHWIEBERT, *Trout Tackle + Two* (1984)

FAVORITE ROD

I was introduced to Vince Cummings fly rods back in the early 1970s by Gardner Grant, an ardent fly-fisherman and advocate of numerous angling organizations. At that time, Gardner was actively involved with Theodore Gordon Flyfishers, Federation of Fly Fishers, Trout Unlimited, and the Atlantic Salmon Federation.

When I met Gardner he had several rods that were made by Vince Cummings, including an eight-foot, two-piece rod that he had me cast one day at the end of a fishing trip to the Delaware River. I liked the rod and the craftsmanship that it exhibited; it had a grip that fit my hand as if it were made-to-order. I asked Gardner if Cummings would make me a one-piece eight-foot rod. I had never thought of the idea of a one-piece rod before–the idea came to me as I was casting.

Vince lived in Westchester County but maintained a shop in Rockland County in Stony Point where he made custom fiberglass fly rods. There are rods that are proficient for casting and others that are best suited for fishing; at times you may even find a rod that casts and fishes equally well. The one-piece Cummings was the best rod I ever owned, and for 47 years it was my rod of choice. It had been a great rod all those years but I didn't want to worry about damaging something that I enjoyed so much, and I retired the rod a few years ago.

Navigating an eight-foot one-piece fly rod in and out of cars, through the woods sometimes in the dark, and along the banks of rivers and streams day after day without an accident is no small achievement. I could not even estimate how many hours I fished with the rod, or how many trout had I caught with it. I replaced and rewound all of the guides three or four times over the years, most likely because I spent an enormous amount of time with the rod on the Delaware River, where long casts are often a must and any trout larger than 14 inches could put you into the backing. The vast majority of the trout were wild, and the fish have room to make long runs with plenty of jumps.

Vince Cummings began his career by making five- and six-strip cane rods and learned much of the trade from Nat Uslan, a cane-rod maker from Rockland County. Vince was known for the fine craftsmanship that he assigned to the custom fiberglass fly-rods he produced. When he received custom-designed glass blanks from the factory he would further refine them by hand, sanding to reduce wall thickness at strategic locations. Known as a master rod builder, Cummings rods had the reputation of being made in the traditions of the finest bamboo.

I was especially fond of the grip, which was finely tapered and different from any I had ever seen. The rod replicates bamboo, is

38. The 1-piece, 8-foot Vince Cummings rod is still my favorite rod.

delicate and light, and without ferrules there are no dead spots. It is easy to feel the line when casting, and in a visceral way the rod assists with casting accurately. It is smooth-flowing when distance is necessary. I used the rod regularly on the big river where distance is often needed and sometimes makes the difference between catching fish or not. The rod has the same assets that a bamboo rod has, and feels like a part of you when it's in your hand. When you hook a trout, you can feel the fish's strength through the rod.

I purchased my one-piece eight-foot Cummings in 1973. I'm not aware of how many others Vince made, but the first person I allowed to try out my rod was Cory Wells. At the time Cory was a lead singer with the rock band Three Dog Night, one of the most successful rock bands of the late 1960s and 1970s, and again in the early 1980s.

My diary records for 1974 revealed that on August 18th Cory phoned and told me the band had just finished a concert in Binghamton, N.Y. and that he had a day off and was anxious to fish the Delaware River.

39. Cory Wells with his 1-piece, 8-foot Vince Cummings rod.

Cory, an avid fisherman, was known for taking his fishing tackle with him when the band was on tour. He was less than an hour's drive from the Delaware River.

We planned to meet at the Circle E diner in Hancock around 4:00 p.m. When we arrived at the river we started walking to a favorite pool, and spooked a deer that scrambled up the bank; and we spotted a bald eagle overhead, slowly making its way down the river. The weather was perfect, and in this part of the Delaware the only audible sounds were made by the river itself. My thoughts were focused on the contrast between the rock star's concert the night before and the natural beauty of the Delaware. Its clear cold water, wildlife, scenic mountains, and peacefulness took effect immediately. "I didn't think there were still places left in New York such as this" said the native of Buffalo.

My diary entry stated:

"Caught 1 wild R.T. (rainbow) 16" Adams #14. Fished from 5 to 9 pm. H2O 69 degrees @5 pm. Not many flies, few #12 all white spinners. Fished with Cory Wells (Three Dog Night.) Cory played in a concert in Binghamton last night and had the day off today. He was broken off twice by large fish; I think he was not used to trout being unrestrained, making long runs and jumps the way Delaware trout do when they are hooked. I thought the rod he had with him was a little stiff and that he would do better with a rod with a more sensitive tip that would bow to the fish if the strike was too quick, so I let him use my one-piece Cummings. With my rod Cory quickly hooked and landed a rainbow between 15"-17." He liked the rod so much that he asked me to order him one like mine."

We corresponded regularly for several years and in one letter Cory sent me a photo of a 20-inch, 4-pound rainbow he caught in the Sierras. In the letter he stated the eight-foot one-piece rod "sure got a good work out this time. It felt good to feel soft glass in my hand again. Vince might be happy to know I still love it. Looking at that rod, it brings back memories of you and me and the Delaware."

Bamboo rods are made by skilled craftsmen who prepare the cane and take great pride in creating a fly rod that allows the angler to enjoy every facet of trout fishing. Because of this, many cane rods have a built-in persona, which gives the angler added delight to their fishing. A bamboo rod feels alive in your hands and obeys your every move; you and the rod can become one. If you are careless when setting the hook by moving the rod too fast, a bamboo rod will bow to the fish and make up for your mistake: so does my one-piece fiberglass Cummings.

My fishing experiences have been greatly enhanced by fishing bamboo and my Cummings rod. Bamboo rods and my Cummings rod aid your timing by letting you feel, through the rod, when the back cast is complete and the line has straightened out, and you know that it's time to begin the forward stroke. The delicacy and flexibility of these rods are like no other, and can build your confidence by improving your casting. Fishing with these rods has contributed to my casting accuracy and presentation of a dry fly. And similar to my one-piece glass rod, when you hook a trout, a bamboo fly rod permits you to feel the strength and energy of the fish.

REEL

All of my life I have read that the reel is the least important part of your equipment, but I disagree. On larger rivers where trout can put you into your backing at almost any time, you should have a reel that will hold a good amount of backing and assist you by letting the fish take line smoothly and evenly. I have used a Hardy Princess reel since the early 1960s. I enjoy the way the reel allows the trout to take line. I also have carried a sinking fly line on an extra spool for fishing wet flies. This saves time in switching from dry-fly to wet-fly fishing. In addition, it saves me the trouble of changing a good dry-fly leader to add on a dropper.

FLY LINES

When it comes to fly lines I do have a couple of eccentric ideas, one of which is that I rarely if ever have fished with anything other than a white double-tapered floating fly line. When I was a teenager in the 1950s, I remember seeing an advertisement in an outdoor magazine that featured a white floating fly line. I believe it was an Ashaway line, and part of the sales promotion was the idea that using a white line was superior to others. It stated that all creatures associated with water were dark on top and white underneath, such as fish, frogs, tadpoles, ducks, and the like, and the reason for this was that the color white protected them from predators below the water. I understood this to mean that a white fly line is harder to detect from below the surface against the sky than colored fly lines, and perhaps it is easier for the angler to see. I still try to use white floating fly lines whenever possible.

Although I have used these lines for many years, they are now more difficult to find. Just a few years ago I went into a local fly shop looking for a white double-tapered floating fly line, only to find that they didn't carry any double-tapered fly lines at all. The last two white lines that I purchased came from England. There is an old saying with fishing equipment, "if you find something you really like, buy a couple of them because they will stop making them."

I prefer to fish with a double-tapered fly line. I use this line in order to present the fly accurately and delicately, and it makes sense to me that since the leader is tapered, the fly line should also be tapered. In addition, with a double-tapered line, you are essentially purchasing two lines for the price of one, as when one end wears out, you turn the line around and use the other end. The lighter front end of a double-tapered fly line offers an easier delivery and plays an essential role in how accurately you cast. My experience with a weight-forward fly line, which has additional weight and thickness on the forward section of the line, is that when you go to check or stop the line when it reaches the target, the line drops on the water awkwardly. A weight-forward line may help you achieve distance with larger and heavier flies, especially on windy days, but a good caster shouldn't need to depend on a weight-forward line.

LEADERS

Although I enjoy using knotless leaders, I found that after changing flies a few times you have no idea if your 6X tippet is cut back to 5X or even 4X. Every time a fly is tied on, more of the tippet is used. Depending on how much of the tippet is left, this can change the diameter and balance of the tippet, and can negatively affect your casting and accuracy in placing the fly. And unless you carry a micrometer you may not know when to replace the tippet.

I have made my own leaders from an Orvis leader kit that I purchased many years ago and when needed, I re-supply the kit as the tippet spools run out. The best part of making your own leaders is that you always know when to add a new section or tippet because the knot is an indication of each section. A good leader is essential to dry-fly presentation.

The tippet must correspond with the size of the fly (hook). One reason for this is that if the hook size is too large for the tippet, the fly can weaken the tippet by spinning or twisting, especially if it is a winged fly; and even if the fly floats and is taken by a fish, the tippet is apt to break. Secondly, if the tippet size is too large for the fly, the fly may not float properly with the wings cocked upright. It may land on its side or even on its head. Matching the hook size to the tippet also holds true for wet flies, nymphs, streamers, and bucktails. Using a #6 streamer on 7X tippet would be difficult to cast, and most likely the first trout that takes the fly will break off. For the vast majority of your trout fishing the following chart should suffice:

TIPPET SIZE	DIAMETER	FLY SIZE
4X	.007	#8 #10 #12
5X	.006	#14 #16 #18
6X	.005	#16 #18
7X	.004	#20 #22
8X	.003	#20 #22

As can be seen there are some overlaps.

The finer the tippet the more natural the fly will look and float. My preference is to tie on one size finer tippet than may be necessary. A size #16 dry fly can be fished with 6X or 5X; however, if you use the 6X it will give the fly a better float.

Common lengths for leaders are 7 1/2 feet, 9 feet, and 12 feet, although I have never found a reason for using 12-foot leaders in the waters I fish. I tend to use a 9-foot leader tapered to 4X. When I wish to fish smaller hook sizes I add on a piece of 5X or 5X and 6X. If I decide to go down to 7X, I tie a section on to the 6X. I use a barrel knot when making a leader at home and a double surgeon's knot when adding tippet in the field.

The specifications I use the most for dry-fly fishing are for a 9-foot 4X leader as follows:

36" - .021	6" - .013
16" - .019	6" - .011
12" - .017	6" - .009
6" - .015	20" - .007

The specifications for a 9-foot, 5X leader:

28" - .021	6" - .011
14" - .019	6" - .009
12" - .017	6" - .007
10" - .015	20" - .006
6" - .013	

When I want to fish 6X or 7X I just add a 20"-to 24" section of tippet to either the 4X or 5X leader. If a wind knot develops on your tippet it is best to stop casting and put on a new tippet; if you hook into a good fish the tippet will break at the knot. A good habit to become accustomed to is to re-tie your fly after you catch a large trout, in the 18 to 20-inch size range. The larger the trout, the larger its teeth, and the tippet may have been frayed or stretched while playing the fish. I have been a victim of not heeding this advice on more than one occasion.

When fishing wet flies, one can usually get away with having the wet-fly leader a little heavier than the corresponding dry-fly leader, such as 4X instead of 5X.

FLIES

Ever since I learned how to tie flies many years ago, I have tied all my own flies and only use flies that I have tied.

With regard to fly dressing, in recent years I have used Mucilin, made in England by Thomas Aspinall, which is generally found in most fly shops. I apply the Mucilin on each fly before I cast it. After catching a fish, I dry the fly off and reapply the Mucilin.

22

CREATING NEW
FLY PATTERNS

*It would seem, with well over a thousand patterns of flies
on the market that we would find it impossible to create anything
new. However, each year brings its new crop of flies; many are
useless, some are useful for a day or two, and some prove to be
consistent producers throughout the season.*

REUBEN R. CROSS, *Fur, Feathers and Steel* (1940)

ZUG BUG ALTERATION

I never really had the urge to create a new fly pattern; although I did
alter the Zug Bug nymph years ago, soon after I started using it; I had
caught a lot of trout on the original fly design, which I learned from
McClane's *Standard Fishing Encyclopedia*. The book contains color
photographs of nearly 200 fly patterns tied by Catskill fly-tiers Harry
and Elsie Darbee.

The pattern given for the Zug Bug as tied by Elsie Darbee in
McClane's *Fishing Encyclopedia* is:

ELSIE DARBEE'S ZUG BUG

HOOK: #12 Mustad #9671 or #9672
THREAD: Black silk 8/0
TAIL: Three strands of peacock sword
BODY: Heavy peacock herl ribbed
RIBBING: Medium silver oval tinsel
WING CASE: Mallard flank feather cut short, over ¼ of the body
HACKLE: Long soft brown
HEAD: Black silk thread
LEAD WIRE (or today's acceptable substitute) is used for weight
    before tying the body; after the lead is wound it is coated
    with lacquer.

The pattern uses heavy or large-size peacock herl found near the eye
of the peacock feather, although not all peacock feathers contain this
large herl. The herl can often be trimmed and shaped after applying
the ribbing, as it tends to move in the water, giving life-like qualities to
the fly. I did not care for the wing case of mallard flank feather, and my
alteration to the pattern substitutes a green teal wing feather instead.

40. My
version of
the Zug Bug
nymph with a
Green Teal
wing case.

41. The Able Mabel dry fly, created in honor of Mabel Ingalls, a founding member of the Woman FlyFishers Club.

THE ABLE MABEL
(A CELEBRATORY DRY FLY)

Some years ago, I was contacted by members of the Woman Flyfishers Club and asked to design a dry fly in the Catskill style.

The Catskill style of dry flies is said to have been created by Theodore Gordon who fashioned some of the first American dry-fly patterns accepted as standards. English dry flies did not float well on streams of rapid descent, and Gordon purposely created a dry fly that would float in fast water. His unique style propelled the craft into an art form that became regional to the Catskills and still exists today.

A Catskill-style fly has a generally sparse appearance: a fine, tapered body of fur or quill; a perfectly matched, divided wing of wood-duck flank feathers; and a sparse, incredibly stiff, glossy hackle, most often blue dun or ginger in various shades.

The fly was needed for the club's 60th Anniversary Dinner in the spring of 1992 and was to honor Mabel Ingalls, a founding member of the Club. The Club, which originally had only eight members, became incorporated in 1932. Membership grew rapidly; in just seven years, it increased more than seven-fold, to fifty-two. The Woman Flyfishers originally maintained a club house at the headwaters of the Willowemoc Creek, and today it is located on the lower Beaverkill downriver from Roscoe.

The fly that I designed was dubbed by club members as the "Able Mabel." The pattern is as follows:

THE ABLE MABEL

HOOK: #12 Mustad 94840
THREAD: Black silk 8/0
WINGS: Flank feathers of a drake wood duck
TAIL: Dark brown or chocolate hackle fibers
BODY: Mink fur dubbing (a few guard hairs left in)
HACKLE: One natural red-brown and one grizzly hackle
    wound together
RIBBING: Amber cotton thread
HEAD: Black silk

Since the pattern was to be in the Catskill style, the wings were made of wood-duck flank feathers, and because I was a big fan of the Adams, I used red-brown and grizzly hackle mixed for the hackle.

I tied the Able Mabel in the early spring of 1992, but I didn't fish with the pattern until late May. The first time I fished with it was on my birthday, near the end of May. I did not intend for the fly to imitate any mayfly, but when I cast the fly on the water it resembled a March Brown riding the surface.

My diary reveals that I fished the lower East Branch in the evening, and caught "1 - 14 ½" wild rainbow, 1 - 19" wild rainbow and 1 - 16" wild brown trout on #12 Able Mabel." I generally do well at this time of the year because it is also prime time for fishing in the Catskills, when fly hatches are abundant and water temperatures are favorable. My notes also state that there was an abundance of "Green Drakes, caddis flies and #18 light-colored mayflies." Green Drakes tend to hatch the last week in May or the first week in June.

THE JOAN WULFF SPECIAL

Thirty years later, in the spring of 2022, the Woman Flyfishers Club celebrated their 90th anniversary, and to commemorate the occasion club members again contacted me to create another Catskill-style dry fly–this time to honor club member Joan Salvato Wulff.

Joan began casting a fly rod in competition when she was just ten years old. Her father Jimmy Salvato was a member of the Paterson Casting Club and introduced Joan to the world of fly-fishing and casting in 1936. One year later Joan began winning club casting competitions and seemed to have found her niche as she continued to win. Joan won sixteen, and won her first national casting competition in the women's dry-fly accuracy championship at the National Association of Angling and Casting Clubs in Chicago. The teenager also competed as an amateur at the nationals in 1944, 1945, and 1946, winning women's dry-fly accuracy in all three years and women's wet-fly accuracy in two of these contests. Between 1943 and 1951 she won twenty-one contests, concluding her amateur career by becoming the first woman to win the National Fisherman's Distance Fly Championship with a long cast of 136 feet against all-male competition.

Joan turned professional and continued winning championships into the 1960s, finishing her casting tournament career with an unofficial world-record cast of 161 feet, in a contest that included men, as there was no women's division at the competition.

In April 1946, the *Pennsylvania Angler* magazine featured a picture of Joan on the cover, credited as Joan Salvato, Paterson, N.J, NATIONAL FLY-CASTING CHAMPION. Joan was nineteen years old at the time.

Many years later, she would sign my copy of the magazine "To Ed with love and admiration for all that you are! Joan Salvato." It is one of my most prized possessions.

The pattern I devised for the Joan Wulff Special is as follows:

THE JOAN WULFF SPECIAL

HOOK: #12 Mustad 94840
THREAD: Black silk 8/0
WINGS: Wood duck flank
TAIL: Light blue dun
BODY: Fox belly fur, cream and gray mixed
HACKLE: Grizzly and light blue dun wound together
HEAD: Black silk

42. The Joan Wulff Special dry fly created in her honor as a long-time member of the Woman Flyfishers Club.

43. Joan and Ed with the Joan Wulff Special fly he created in her honor for the Woman FlyFishers Club 90th Anniversary.

2 3

ONE OF THE JOYS

> *How shall I describe that wild, beautiful stream*
> *with features so like those of all other mountain streams? . . .*
> *The solitude was perfect; and I felt that strangeness and*
> *insignificance which the civilized man must always feel when*
> *opposing himself to such a vast scene of silence and wildness.*
>
> JOHN BURROUGHS, *Speckled Trout,*
> *Atlantic Monthly* (October 1870)

There are times during the season when I seek out places to fish to enjoy the solitude and satisfaction one receives by discovering new waters that contain wild trout. Although I most often fish the larger streams and rivers, I do enjoy going on a sojourn occasionally into the Catskill Forest Preserve.

There are almost 300,000 acres of state-owned forest land that remain by law "forever wild." These lands are open to the public for outdoor activities such as fishing, hunting, hiking, cross-country skiing, and camping. A great deal of this forest land is in the same primal condition that it has always been, with many miles of trout streams as well as lakes and ponds that also contain brook trout.

I am often asked about brook trout, even though it is a rare stream in the Catskills that does not contain these native species. They are more sensitive to water temperatures than either brown or rainbow trout, and when water temperatures begin to rise on the larger streams or rivers in May and June, brook trout often retreat into nearby tributaries.

One of the joys of trout fishing in the Forest Preserve is that native brook trout can still be found in these waters that are unspoiled, with clean, cold, well-oxygenated water. These water courses are mostly streams of rapid descent composed of fragmented rock, boulders, sand, and gravel, with a backdrop of picturesque scenery, and the awe-inspiring beauty of nature.

Trout streams are vibrant, and flyfishers often seek more than trout when they go fishing; they look for solace in the natural world of the stream. They may enjoy the chatter of a kingfisher, and the gobble of a wild turkey perched on a limb letting others know it is ready to leave the roost. Or they may take delight in the sight of a doe nursing a fawn while standing in the middle of the stream; I witnessed this scene more than fifty years ago and still think of it.

There is pleasure in hiking into a trout stream or pond that you may not have seen before; the scenery is original and so are the native brook trout! Often you will have the stream to fish all to yourself. On occasions, you may have to share the stream with a beaver. While beavers do not eat fish, they do have an impact on the waters they share with brook trout. The most beautiful of the trout species found in the Catskills, these small wild jewels of the headwaters sport an olive-green body outlined by white, black, and orange-edged fins and punctuated by yellow and blue-rimmed red spots.

Beavers, which are common on Forest Preserve lands, can improve trout habitat, especially in places where it is needed. A beaver dam constructed across the stream raises the water upstream of the dam and deepens the water downstream of the dam by scouring out a small plunge pool. Beavers often provide additional pools or ponds along forest streams in this way, giving trout more space and depth and consequently more food, which allows brook trout the opportunity to grow larger than average. (Along small streams a rule of nature dictates that the size and depth of the pools corresponds with the size of the trout: the larger the pool, the larger the fish.)

Some of the best trout fishing I have ever enjoyed occurred in small streams where beavers had created ponded water. I remember a beaver pond that I found at the source of a stream. The pond had a healthy population of brook trout that measured in the 11 to 12-inch range, while those below the dam were typically 7 or 8 inches.

I look forward to fishing a particular Forest Preserve stream once or twice each year that contains a series of beaver dams, one after another, for more than a mile. The beaver dams keep this low-gradient stream filled with water throughout that section; and it contains an abundance of native brook trout.

Although brook trout tend to be the dominant species throughout the Forest Preserve, I have on occasion found waters containing native brown and rainbow trout. However, I think it's safe to say that the majority of streams in the preserve are predominantly native brook trout water.

A special feature found along many streams in the Forest Preserve is the presence of waterfalls, which offer unequaled natural beauty and present a portrait of nature at its finest, with no two waterfalls looking exactly the same. Waterfalls are the part of the stream that speak the loudest. They announce their whereabouts via the sound of rushing water plummeting over a ledge of bedrock. And they also provide a dividend with the best accommodations for the trout. Waterfalls are inclined to create a plunge pool of added depth and space, as well as more highly oxygenated water. The habitat created by waterfalls can become the throne of the largest trout in the stream.

I was reminded of such a trout I had encountered long ago. It was recorded in my angling diary on September 10, 1979, that I was fishing the upper Esopus Creek on Forest Preserve land. I came across a

44. A beautiful brook trout, typical of the wild fish found in the Catskill Forest Preserve.

cascading waterfall that split the stream into separate channels as the water flowed around a bend. It surged over solid rock ledges, united, and then plunged into a spacious, deep pool, crafting excellent trout habitat.

I was able to work my way to the rim of a rock ledge that was about 20 feet above the plunge pool. This enabled me to get a clear look into the translucent water, where I watched trout of various sizes leisurely swimming around. While planning my strategy on how to land a fish, I soon realized that I would have difficulty hoisting anything up to where I was other than a small trout. Because the pool was deep with a slow flow, I decided to tie on a size #12 weighted Zug Bug nymph. Its thick peacock-herl body would appear life-like; the herl would provide movement in the slow water.

I lowered the Zug Bug into the water, and even before I moved the fly, an 8-inch brook trout grabbed it. I set the hook and, almost immediately, a large brown trout seized the brook trout, held it sideways in its sizable mouth and began swimming around the pool with the tip of the brook trout's tail protruding from one side of its jaw, and the head out the opposite side! The large fish had a firm grip on the brook trout and shook it as a dog would a toy. I realized there was no way I would be able to hoist the large brown twenty feet in the air, so I began leading the fish slowly up toward the surface, hoping that the brown would just release the smaller fish. It did so, but not before I had raised the larger fish's head, still clinging to the brook trout, partially out of the water. As I continued to reel the brook trout, minus his captor, up out of the water to where I was standing on the ledge, I could see that there was no life left in it. I believed the large brown deserved the smaller fish and tossed it back into the pool. I generally try not to overestimate the sizes of trout when I cannot measure them, but I estimated that the brown that grabbed the brook trout was at least 17 or 18 inches in length.

45. One of the joys found in fishing in the Catskill Forest Preserve.

Many of these Forest Preserve streams were fished by the naturalist John Burroughs back in the 1860s-1890s. In his book *In the Catskills* (1910) Burroughs states:

> *The fisherman has a harmless, preoccupied, look; he is a vagrant that nothing fears. He blends himself with the trees and the shadows. All his approaches are gentile and indirect. He times himself to the meandering soliloquizing stream; he addresses himself to it till he knows its hidden secrets. Where it deepens, his purpose deepens; where it is shallow he is in-different. He knows how to interpret its every glance and dimple; its beauty haunts him for days.*

During my research on Burroughs some years back, I was able to view his diaries at Vassar College, and was interested to read about his fishing experiences and exactly where he fished. Later that summer I fished some of the same streams that Burroughs had fished as a youngster and as an adult, and found that these waters still contain native

brook trout. At the headwaters of the Beaverkill and tributaries of the East Branch of the Delaware and the West Branch of the Neversink River, there are still native brook trout today as there were in his day.

Outside of the Forest Preserve, private forested land can be changed: re-shaped with heavy machinery by removing trees to create meadows or farmland, and nature does not react noticeably to these changes. Over the passage of time, if this "improved" land is abandoned, it will revert back to what it was–forest land.

However, streams and rivers are different: you cannot create good habitat or improve a trout stream with a bulldozer or excavator. Changes to flow patterns can have the opposite effect to what was intended. Good habitat can be destroyed unintentionally, and disruption to the bottom substrate can affect the waters upstream and down. In addition, the bottom-living creatures and aquatic insects will be destroyed in the process.

Streams are dynamic entities of power and energy; they are self-motivated, and rise and fall with weather patterns. Today they are more erratic, due to climate change, than at any other time in our past. Man's attempts to manipulate these flowing waters often fails, which is perhaps the best possible outcome of seeking to disrupt natural habitat, and ultimately destroying one of the joys of fishing.

24

END NOTE

When I started to write this book, I believed that I was going to learn from the experience primarily how or why I was able to catch trout on just a few different fly patterns, whether dry or wet or nymph imitations. Before I began reviewing my diaries, I believed that most of my success was the result of having used the Adams dry fly, and mainly because of the way I tied the fly. I thought that reviewing the diaries would provide a definitive answer.

Inside my fly box are flies that match hatches, as well as a few standard fly patterns that do not. Interestingly, right from the beginning I had more success with fly patterns that did not imitate anything specific in nature, such as the Adams, Pheasant-Tail Midge, Chuck Caddis, and Royal Wulff dry flies. My choice of using fewer rather than more dry-fly patterns increased when I began recording my trout-fishing experiences.

In writing this book I realized that my success in fly-fishing was due to a complexity of things and not any one in particular. I now believe there was more to my success than just the fly. In fact, my vision plays a role, at least with dry-fly fishing, in that seeing your fly and the fish rising is a major component to successful fly-fishing.

I knew how to double-haul before realizing what a double-haul was; I think I just figured it out myself. Once I learned to double-haul, I was now fishing with two hands rather than just one, and it improved my accuracy and distance in casting the dry fly. In most instances, if you know how to double-haul, it makes you a better caster; I believe this is the epitome of good casting. You can reach more fish with more skill. I knew that I could cast for distance, and that I was able to place the fly where I wanted it to go.

I also realized that I fished a great deal more often than most people. Having been able to fish almost every day of the season gave me a lot of time on the water, learning where to fish and when to fish, improving my casting as well as how best to set the hook. I was quick but not too quick, and rarely did I leave a fly in a fish or break off.

With that added time on the water, I perfected my casting to where I could straighten out and lay the line low to the water and, coupled with having good vision, was able to make fewer false casts in order to hit the "target."

I also credit the type of rod I used: bamboo or soft glass. I tend to shy away from the latest fads or fly-fishing trends and have used a 5- or 6-weight double-tapered white fly line most of my life.

I prefer to use flies that are tied with natural materials rather than synthetic, and always expect the fish to take the fly on the first cast. When presenting the fly I fish with confidence–and put the fly on a "collision course" with the fish so that the fish "has" to take it.

These reasons have enabled me to fish with confidence–and I believe that fishing with confidence is a key in catching fish and being successful in fly-fishing.

SOME FAVORITE BOOKS

Art Flick
Art Flick's New Streamside Guide
Crown Publishers, Inc., 1969

Charles K. Fox
This Wonderful World of Trout
Foxcrest, 1963

Charles K. Fox
Rising Trout
Foxcrest, 1967

Arnold Gingrich
American Trout Fishing
Alfred A. Knopf, 1966

Roderick L. Haig-Brown
A River Never Sleeps
Crown Publishers, Inc., 1974

John Waller Hills
A History of Fly Fishing
Freshet Press, 1972

George Parker Holden
Streamcraft: An Angling Manual
Stewart & Kidd Co., 1919

Preston Jennings
A Book of Trout Flies
Crown Publishers, Inc., 1970

J. Edson Leonard
The Essential Fly Tier
Prentice-Hall, Inc., 1976

Norman Maclean
A River Runs Through It
University of Chicago Press, 1976

A. J. McClane
Fishing with McClane
Prentice-Hall, Inc., 1975

A. J. McClane
The Practical Fly Fisherman
Prentice-Hall, Inc., 1975

John McDonald
The Complete Fly Fisherman:
    The Notes and Letters of
    Theodore Gordon
Nick Lyons Books, 1989

J. Michael Migel and
    Leonard M. Wright, Jr.
The Masters on the Nymph
Nick Lyons Books, 1979

Chas. M. Wetzel
Practical Fly Fishing
The Christopher Publishing
    House, 1943

Joan Wulff
Joan Wulff's Fly-Casting Accuracy
The Lyons Press, 1997

Lee Wulff
Trout on a Fly
Nick Lyons Books, 1986

Lee Wulff
Lee Wulff on Flies
Stackpole Books, 1980

PHOTO AND
FLY TYER CREDITS

00. Ed Van Put photo
01. Lee Van Put photo, Mosquito fly tied by Ed Van Put
02. Lee Van Put photo, April Gray fly tied by Judy Van Put
03. Lee Van Put photo
04. Judy Van Put photo
05. Chart by Lee Van Put
06. Chart by Lee Van Put
07. Lee Van Put photo, Chuck Caddis fly tied by Judy Van Put
08a. Lee Van Put photo, Royal Coachman fly tied by Ed Van Put
08b. Lee Van Put photo, Royal Wulff fly tied by Seth Cavarretta
09. Ed Van Put photo
10. Ed Van Put photo
11. Lee Van Put photo, fly tied by Ed Van Put
12. Ed Van Put photo
13. Lionel Atwill photo
14. Lee Van Put photo, Flying Caddis Fly tied by Ed Van Put
15. Lee Van Put photo, Adams fly tied by Ed Van Put
16. Lee Van Put photo, Pheasant-Tail Midge fly tied by Ed Van Put
17. Lee Van Put photo
18. Lee Van Put photo March Brown Spider fly tied by Tom Mason
19. Gordon Allen illustration
20. Lee Van Put photo, Orange Fish Hawk fly tied by Ed Van Put

21. Ed Van Put photo
22. Lee Van Put photo Royal
    Coachman wet fly tied by
    Ed Van Put
23. Lee Van Put photo Leadwing
    Coachman fly tied by Ed
    Van Put
24. Lee Van Put photo, Vamp
    streamer fly tied by Ed
    Van Put
25. Gordon Allen illustration
26. Lee Van Put photo, Blue
    Quill fly tied by Ed Van Put
27. Judy Van Put photo
28. Ed Van Put photo
29. Kris Lee photo
30. Ed Van Put photo, Don Roth
    with 20+ inch hallmark trout
31. Kris Lee photo

32. Charts by Ed Van Put
33. Phil Chase photo
34. Phil Chase photo
35. Phil Chase photo
36. Shelly Rustin photo
37. Lee Van Put photo
38. Christian Anwander photo
39. Photo Courtesy of Cory Wells
40. Lee Van Put photo, Zug Bug
    fly tied by Ed Van Put
41. Lee Van Put photo, Able
    Mabel fly tied by Ed Van Put
42. Lee Van Put photo, Joan
    Wulff Special fly tied by Ed
    Van Put
43. Judy Van Put photo
44. Ed Van Put photo
45. Ed Van Put photo